Postmodernism

Postmodernism

What You Should Know and Do About It

(2nd Edition)

Robert Brewer

Writer's Showcase
New York   Lincoln   Shanghai

Postmodernism
What You Should Know and Do About It

All Rights Reserved © 2002 by Robert Kent Brewer

No part of this book may be reproduced or transmitted in any form or by any means, graphic, electronic, or mechanical, including photocopying, recording, taping, or by any information storage retrieval system, without the written permission of the publisher.

Writer's Showcase
an imprint of iUniverse, Inc.

For information address:
iUniverse
2021 Pine Lake Road, Suite 100
Lincoln, NE 68512
www.iuniverse.com

ISBN: 0-595-25372-5 (Pbk)
ISBN: 0-595-65130-5 (Cloth)

Printed in the United States of America

To Kristen, my wife, soul-mate, companion, and forever love.

To Mom & Dad, Thanks for your unconditional love.

Contents

Foreword ix
Preface xiii

Part I—Understanding The Postmodernist Culture

Chapter 1—How In The Worldview Did We Get Here? 3
Chapter 2—It's All Relative…Isn't It? 14
Chapter 3—Ignorance Of Christian Beliefs 19
Chapter 4—A Pluralistic Conspiracy 24
Chapter 5—Suspicious Minds 32
Chapter 6—Spiritual Curiousity 37

Part II—Postmodern Entertainment

Chapter 7—Popcorn & Postmodernism 43
Chapter 8—Postmodern Art 47

Part III—Prerequisites For Postmodern Ministry

Chapter 9—No Compromise 53
Chapter 10—Intentional Evangelism 62
Chapter 11—Postmodern Apologetics 71
Chapter 12—Know Your Culutre, Know Your Niche 90
Chapter 13—Utilizing The Personal Testimony 100
Chapter 14—Building Relationships 103
Chapter 15—Getting Global, Getting Local 106

Conclusion 111
Bibliography 113
Appendix: What is the Gospel? 123
About the Author 125

Foreword

Postmodernism is a word that is currently used by many ministers in their sermons that most people on the street do not understand. It's a term that means everything, and at the same time nothing. As a result, most people are confused when they hear the word postmodernism.

Dr. Bobby Brewer has helped people understand what it is, how it affects the church, and what the church can do about it.

When Bobby was a student at Liberty University, not only was he an outstanding student; he had a passion for ministry that involved preaching, evangelism and ministering to individuals. He brings that passion to this topic, and through the pages of this manuscript he continues to evangelize, preach and minister to people.

Dr. Brewer has explained that when culture changes, the first thing the church must do is to be willing to adjust outreach methods. Our beliefs are eternal, and the content of our ministry never changes; so we must hold fast to our beliefs in a changing culture more than ever. However, when culture changes, so should our outreach methods. This does not mean that we change our principles, but rather; we change our methods. Our principles are eternally timeless, and they remain transculturally the same. The principles of the Word of God will work in any day, and they will work in any culture. Our principles will work even in the new postmodern culture that's arrived. However, methods will always change because *methods are the adaptation of principles to culture.*

> Methods are many,
> Principles are few;
> Methods may change,
> But principles never do.

As we build good relationships with the unchurched postmodern, and we use our testimony as a tool to share the gospel; we must always give honor to the Lord Jesus Christ who is the center of our faith.

Postmodernism is more than the changes in the way people dress, act, and live. Postmodernism reflects a change in the way people think. As they once thought rationally, now they tend to think viscerally. In the past they used logic to arrive at faith, but the postmodernist sees logic as irrelevant. Postmoderns feel that they are not holding the truth, telling the truth, or believing the truth that is eternal. But to them truth is not an eternal absolute, but rather a pragmatic way to think. The postmodern person may say, "I believe that abortion is wrong; however, my good friend was right to get an abortion because someone she did not love impregnated her."

To the postmodern, words do not have meaning. Words only mean what the current user attributes to them. That is because truth is not eternal. It is only relative. To the postmodern, truth only means what is agreed upon, or that which has been attributed to by the user. However, when you know that the Word of God is eternal, and that God is eternal, then you know that truth is eternal, and morality is eternal.

> IF THERE IS NO ABSOLUTE TRUTH,
>   THERE IS NO ABSOLUTE MORALITY.
> IF THERE IS NO ABSOLUTE STANDARD,
>   THEN THERE IS NO SIN.
> IF THERE IS NO TRANSGRESSION,
>   THEN THERE IS NO NEED FOR A SAVIOR.
> IF WE DO NOT NEED SALVATION,
>   THEN THERE IS NO NEED FOR JESUS CHRIST.
> IF JESUS CHRIST IS NOT NECESSARY,
>   THEN WHY THE CHURCH?

However, we have an everlasting gospel to preach (Rev. 14:6). "His truth endureth to all generations" (Psa.100: 5). God is eternal who does not change. Inasmuch, God is the same from one generation to another, and from one changing culture to another.

This book will help us understand culture, and help to adapt our unchanging message to a changing world. May we all study it, and understand the times, and reach people for Jesus Christ.

Sincerely yours in Christ,

Elmer L. Towns, Dean
School of Religion
Liberty University
Lynchburg, Virginia

Preface

"No." was the student's reply when asked if he believed in absolute truth. I was a part of team of eight that had been invited to conduct some "spiritual surveys" for an upcoming outreach event with Ravi Zacharias in Moscow. Wendy, the co-leader of the team tried again by asking the Math major, "Would you agree that if 20 students take a math exam and they each write twenty different answers that they could not all be right?" Once again he politely said, "No." "So, 2 + 2 could = 5?" she quizzically asked. "Maybe. There are so many different answers to everything. You cannot always know for certain."

Like most people, when I first heard about postmodernism, I thought that it was absolutely the most ridiculous and ludicrous worldview I had ever encountered. Initially, it sounded like just another meaningless mind game hatched by some French intellectual types like Foucault and Baudrillard. However, I've learned that postmodernism is a reaction to the most profound spiritual and philosophical crises of our time and very indicative of the spiritual status of contemporary North America. Likewise, it cannot be denied that postmodernism is having a far-reaching impact on the Christian faith, particularly in the West.

As David Bosh said, "Since the seventeenth century more and more people have discovered, originally to their surprise, that they could ignore God and the church, yet be none the worse for it."[1] In the course of time this has led to a common separation of Christianity from its culture in which Christianity's influence and respect have suffered a slow but certain loss of ability to significantly sway culture and worldviews.

---

[1] David Bosch, *Believing in the Future* (Harrisburg, PA: Trinity Press, 1995), p. 15.

After discovering the implications of a postmodern society, I was frustrated to discover that the vast majority of ministry resources, especially in the area of personal evangelism and church growth, were *not* geared towards reaching the postmodern culture. Furthermore, although I found a number of excellent books and resources on postmodernism, searching for information on how to effectively permeate it with the gospel was similar to searching for the proverbial needle in a haystack. This was rather discouraging, because I'm more of a "how-to" type of person and know that most of my peers are too. Simply put, after understanding the major implications of postmodernism I wanted to know what to do about it…fast.

Interestingly, it was during this same period that I was asked by some teen-agers, "What exactly is postmodernism and what should we be doing about it?" Thus, over a cheeseburger and fries during lunch, I did my best at providing an overview of this worldview and its implications for Christianity. Minus the burger and fries, the following is an overview of some of the primary tenets that you should know and understand about postmodernism and how to evangelistically interact within it.

Part I
Understanding The Postmodernist Culture

"But I don't want to go among mad people,"
Alice remarked.
"Oh, you can't help that," said the cat. "We're all mad here. I'm mad. You're mad."
"How do you know I'm mad?" said Alice.
"You must be," said the cat, "or you wouldn't have come here."

—Lewis Carrol, *Alice's Adventures in Wonderland*

Chapter 1

How In The Worldview Did We Get Here?

Peter Drucker says:

> Every few hundred years in Western history there occurs a sharp transformation. We cross what...I have called a 'divide.' Within a few short decades society rearranges itself-its worldview; its basic values; its social and political structure; its arts; its key institutions. Fifty years later, there is a new world. And the people born then cannot even imagine the world in which their grandparents lived and into which their own parents were born...We are currently living through such a transformation.[2]

Paradigm shifts in culture often produce anxiety and uncertainty. As a result of postmodernism, new questions about evangelistic encounters with the North American culture have also emerged. Due to our heritage and resources, we are in a good position to become the best-organized and

---

[2] Peter Drucker, *Post Capitalist Society* (NY: Harper Collins, 1993), p. 1.

most strategic mission in the history of Christianity, if we can develop a missional ethos that's also applicable for our new culture. Cross-cultural missionaries often spend years studying the culture and language of the people-group they aspire to evangelize prior to embarking on a mission. "A missionary or anthropologist who really hopes to understand and enter the adopted culture will not do so by trying to learn the language in the way a tourist uses a phrase book and dictionary. It must be learned in the way a child learns to speak…by learning to think and speak in the way the people of the country do."[3]

Likewise, it's time for the local church in North America to become a student of its culture and learn to speak *postmodernese*. As James Sire said, "[We need to] think in terms of worldviews, that is, with a consciousness, so that we can first understand and then genuinely communicate with others in our pluralistic society."[4] Therefore, like a missionary, it is essential that we first have a good understanding of the postmodern mindset and culture that we seek to evangelize and minister to.

> "Most people catch their presuppositions from their family and surrounding society the way a child catches measles. But people with more understanding realize that their presuppositions should be chosen after a more careful consideration of what worldview is true." Frances Schaeffer

---

[3] Lesslie Newbigin, *The Gospel in a Pluralistic Society* (Grand Rapids: Eerdmans, 1989), p. 56.
[4] James Sire, *The Universe Next Door* (Downers Grove: InterVarsity Press, 1976), p. 15

An Overview of Worldview Developments[5]
Premodernism

To understand our present condition it is helpful to first understand where we came from and how we got here. The premodern worldview believed that the universe was the playground of God or gods. Life was beyond human control and could only be explained in supernatural terms. This period is generally dated from the beginnings of recorded history through the late 17th century. (However, sociologically premodern cultures do still exist in some parts of the earth in which there is little or no cultural or religious diversity, minimal social change, and have not been affected by developments in science or Western secularization). The New Testament church was birthed during this period and even became prevalent when Emperor Constantine came to power in the fourth century making Christianity (and Theism) the predominant worldview for most of the Western world.

In the West, up to the end of the seventeenth century, the theistic worldview was clearly dominant. James Sire said:

> "Intellectual squabbles…were mostly family squabbles. Dominicans might disagree with Jesuits, Jesuits with Anglicans, Anglicans with Presbyterians, ad infinitum, but all these parties subscribed to the same set of basic presuppositions. The triune personal God of the Bible existed; he had revealed himself to us and could be known; the universe was his creation; human

---

[5] A worldview is a set of presuppositions which may be true, false, or a blend of both that a person holds (consciously or subconsciously), about the makeup of the world, life, God, etc. These views are not just limited to the eras described here, but extend into religion, philosophy, sociology, etc. It is also noteworthy that Polytheism was widely practiced in the first half of the premodern period but waned in influence following the rapid spread of Christianity. James Sire, for example, refers to this period as the age of the "Theistic worldview." James Sire, *The Universe Next Door*, p. 22.

beings were his special creation. If battles were fought, the lines were drawn within the circle of theism."[6]

The idea of God's absolute power and authority over all human life formed the foundation for the premodern worldview. Augustine of Hippo (354–430), for example, would champion the belief that God reigned supreme over both church and state with the state existing for the purpose of enforcing moral structures in society.[7] Thus, this era was a uniquely religious culture in which God was intimately involved in every facet of the human experience. The source of all truth and the path to all knowledge was exclusively through divine revelation. In this era, all human reasoning was subject to validation against theology and/or Scripture.

> "We are living on a cultural fault line between two epochal periods."
> —Chuck Smith, Jr.

Modernism

Modernity (1517–1972[8]) introduced the Renaissance, which removed God as the exclusive source of cultural, theological, and philosophical influence. The goal of this era, as Alasdair MacIntyre has indicated, was to free humanity from superstition and found a philosophy and civilization on rational inquiry, empirical evidence and scientific discovery.[9] From a

---

[6] James Sire, *Ibid*, p. 21.
[7] Samuel Stumpf, *Socrates to Sartre, Vol. 4*, (New York: McGraw-Hill, 1988), p. 144.
[8] The date for the end of modernity and beginning of postmodernity is debatable. Nevertheless, the Protestant Reformation and the destruction of the Pruitt-Igoe complex in 1972 is are prudent dates. For a detailed overview on the history of philosophy see Francis Schaeffer's *How Should We Then Live*.
[9] Alasdair MacIntyre, *After Virtue: A Study in Moral Theory*, 2nd ed. (Notre Dame, IN: Univ of Notre Dame Press, 1984).

practical standpoint, humanity and reason were inserted in the place of God. God was still very important, but no longer the center or catalyst of this era's worldview.

Ironically, modern philosophy grew up in the shadow of Christianity. Christianity was, after all, the religious environment that philosophers like Rene Descartes, David Hume, and Friederich Nietzsche all grew up in. It was also Christianity that was to be proved or disproved by Enlightenment thinkers as they applied the best tools that rationalism and science could offer. This period was distinguished by several significant scientific discoveries that shattered several long-held ideas about the universe. Nicholas Copernicus (1473–1543) and Galileo (1564–1647) proved that the universe did not revolve around the earth, but that in fact the earth rotated around the Sun, as did the other planets. This was in direct opposition to the Ptolemic model that had the earth at the center of the universe and thus implying that human beings had a very special place. Therefore, the proposal of the heliocentric model was perceived as an attack against God. The "church" (Roman Catholic) immediately condemned these views, pitting itself against the emerging scientific community and creating a conflict from which it has yet to recover.

The influence of Modernism primarily infiltrated the church through Deism. Deism emphasized the authority of reason in all matters and envisioned a Christianity that was devoid of superstition and irrationality. While it is true that Deists tended to be skeptical towards miracles and special revelation, only the more extremists completely discarded the supernatural. In fact most deists considered themselves to be Christians and felt that they were aiding and advancing Christianity by making it more intellectually palatable by demythologizing it. Some, like John Toland, felt that sacrificing the intellect by accepting the supernatural and mysterious at face value was a violation of the gift of the image of God, which includes the gift of reason. (In fact, Isaac Newton, Rene Descartes, John Locke, and even Thomas Jefferson were very interested in religious and theological questions).

The problem, however, was the fact that all Deists tended to elevate human reason over revelation. Locke treated Christianity purely from an intellectual standpoint. He believed that "whatever God has revealed is true and must be the object of our faith; but what actually counts as having been by God, *that must be judged by reason*" [emphasis mine].[10] Thus, as one Christian historian has said, "[F]or Locke nothing could be a divine revelation that is rejected by reason."[11]

Likewise, when Isaac Newton (1642–1727) established that the universe operated according to certain well-established laws, the "church" was again indirectly dethroned as the primary link between God and humanity. Charles Darwin's publication of the *Origin of Species* in 1859 was probably the final nail in the coffin in the shift towards reason over God. His theory of evolution fueled the visionary enthusiasm of those who saw reason and science as the true saviors.

The predominate outcome was a fundamental tenet of the "Great Enlightenment" that the only reliable knowledge is that which has achieved mathematical clarity and objectivity through reason guided by scientific method. Anything outside of these boundaries, including Christianity, is to be regarded as subjective and open to doubt.[12]

Once this duality of knowledge and truth became accepted, humanity had fully transitioned into the age of modernity. The Enlightenment finished off what the Renaissance and the scientific revolution had begun with its primary belief that a single truth does indeed exist and that human beings are engaged in a journey to discover that single truth. In the

---

[10] John Locke, *A Discourse in Miracles*, ed. I.T. Ramsey (London: Black, 1958), p. 84
[11] Roger Olson, *The Story of Christian Theology* (Downers Grove, IL: InterVarsity Press, 1999), p. 527
[12] Immanuel Kant (1724-1804) was one of the premiere philosophers during this period and may have captured the general ethos of the Enlightenment in his "Dare to know" motto, which encouraged the skepticism of all beliefs in the name of rationality. "(His) philosophy is marked by skepticism and a loss of faith in both religion and metaphysics...Yet, in the face of this overwhelming demolition of traditional beliefs,

Modern worldview, the human mind, not God, provided the logical starting places for this search. The principal characteristic of this age was its complete confidence in humanity and the human mind. Reason and science became the new saviors that could solve humanity's problems and lead us towards a utopian society.

The United States emerged out of this era. Although the first English settlement was in Jamestown, Virginia in 1607, many of these settlers were possibly more influenced by premodern, rather than modern thought. Likewise, many of the settlements were the direct result of an attempt to escape religious institutional persecution. Thus, North America possessed a Christian culture that served as the foundation for the religious worldview of the American people and was predominantly characterized as Protestant.

Along with the Christian faith, Americans were *also* influenced by rationalism and scientific progress. Just as Protestantism largely dominated the religious scene, European Enlightenment dominated the arena of philosophy and the United States emerged with these two foundational views of reality. This unique cultural reality enabled Christianity to establish itself as the source of the grand story (or metanarrative) by which most Americans interpreted their lives. In time, it became bound to the American story and the nation largely believed "Manifest Destiny" and that it was "marked and chosen by the finger of God."[13] "The nation's families, schools, and churches became storytellers who preserved the

---

Kant's philosophy develops a new and profound sense of affirmation. It affirms the *limits* of human knowledge and the creative possibilities resulting form an acknowledgement of these limits. In place of superstition and dogma, Kant embraces change and human fallibility…Such an outlook exceeds modernism's desire for order and progress and places Kant's thought within the turmoil of the postmodern." Christopher Want, *Introducing Kant*, (New York: Totem Books, 1996), p. 3.

[13] John Rolfe, *A Relation of the State of Virginia* (1616) in the Virginia Historical Register and Literary Adviser, quoted in Perry Miller, *Errand to the Wilderness* (Cambridge: Harvard Univ. Press, 1956), p. 119.

truth of the story and ensured its transmission from generation to generation."[14]

The twentieth century began, in the Western world, with a pervasive sense of optimism. Buildings continued to soar upward, railroads and steamships made the world more accessible, and telephones transformed communication. Western societies had every reason to assume that they were on the verge of reaching the highest levels of social, cultural, and technical achievement. These advancements made it natural and fitting to trust in the reliability of human reason…at least until World War I. World War II would force Western civilization to acknowledge that the industrial, scientific, and technological revolutions of modernity had not advanced civilization to a new threshold of utopia. Rather than facing a steady, well-reasoned, upward movement of history that will end in a global utopian civilization, by the 1950s it was clear that the entire planet faced the potential threat of self-destruction.[15]

> "We live in an insecure world, a world threatened by violence, lack, and spiritual malaise…Increasing uncertainty, family violence, cancer…a diminished outlook for all"
> —**Sharif Abdullah**

Postmodernism (1972–Present)

The 20th century, to the postmodernist, was anything but the utopia that was envisioned by the rational thinkers of the Modern era. In fact,

---

[14] Robert Nash, Jr., *An 8-Track Church in a CD World*, p. 28.
[15] In *True and Only Heaven: Progress and Its Critics*, (New York: W.W. Norton, 1991, reprint edition), Christopher Lasch's articulates a similar concern in which he demonstrates that "progress" through materialism and consumerism is basically an illusion that ultimately becomes a society's demise.

not only are they disillusioned by the primary tenets of modernism, they treat its concepts with contempt.

To quote one postmodern author,

> "Besides, what did Science, Reason and Progress get us, after all? The 20th century turned out to be nothing if not a dark, Kafkaesque nightmare of rationally administered death camps, death squads, Auschwitz, World Wars 1 and 2, Hiroshima, Nagasaki, ecological disaster-and various systems of totalitarianism. And all in the name of the Enlightenment values of Science, Reason, Liberation, Freedom and Progress."[16]

Dr. Paul Feyeraberd, professor of Philosophy at the University of California-Berkeley simply says, "Western ideals of progress are damaging sociologically and ecologically."[17]

Charles Jencks, and other architects believe that the postmodern era began on July 15, 1972 at 3:32 p.m. when the Pruitt-Igoe housing development in St. Louis, Missouri, a prize-winning complex designed for low-income people, was dynamited as uninhabitable.[18] "According to Jencks, this proclaimed the death of the *International Style* of modernist architecture, the end of buildings as 'machines for living' envisioned by Mies van

---

[16] Jim Powell, *Postmodernism for Beginners* (New York: Writers & Readers Inc., 1998), p. 10.

[17] Paul Feyerbard, *Farewell to Reason* (New York: Verso, 1987), back cover.

[18] Technically, a true postmodernist would dispute the very idea of unilinear history because postmodernism cannot follow in sequence after modernism because this would be an admission of historic progress and a relapse into "Grand Narrative mythology." It is also noteworthy that the student riots of Paris and the United States in 1968 is another popular reference point for the beginning of the postmodern era due to the fact that their resistance against the "knowledge industry" led poststructural analysts to begin theorizing about the postmodern condition.

der Rohe, Rropius, Le Corbusier and other abstract functionalists."[19] (In fact, the term *postmodernism* is also a reference to an architectural trend that moved away from the practical and unadorned motifs towards complex and impractical ones).[20]

However, postmodernism is obviously much more than just a new trend in architecture. The developments in architecture and construction are merely a reflection of cultural developments. James Sire said,

> "...in the final analysis, postmodernism is not 'post' anything; it is the last move of the modern, the result of the modern taking its own commitments seriously and seeing that they fail to stand the test of analysis. I cannot catalog postmodernism as I have earlier worldviews. Even more than existentialism, postmodernism is both more than and less than a worldview. In major part this is due to the origin of the term within the discipline of sociology rather than philosophy."[21]

On a practical level, everything seems broken to the typical Gen-Xer.[22] The environment seems ruined and possibly beyond repair. Sex isn't fun anymore because of AIDS, and marriage is a very high risk venture that only has a 50% chance of success. These factors aid in making postmodernism the philosophy and lifestyle of choice for today's generation.

Although many recognize that various precursors to postmodernism began to show up in the early twentieth century, the primary changes have

---

[19] Richard Appignanesi, *Introducing Postmodernism* (New York: Totem Books, 1995), p. 115.
[20] Powell, *Postmodernism for Beginners*, pp. 88- 90.
[21] James Sire, *The Universe Next Door*, p. 173-174.
[22] Broadly defined, Generation X, also referred to as Busters, were born between 1965-1983 and represent approximately 66 million Americans.

taken place within the past thirty years. [23] Interestingly and appropriately, it seems that everyone has their *own version* of what the key catalyst was for the ushering in of this new era.

> "Frederick Jameson suggests that the postmodern shift is rooted primarily in the recent transition in our economy to a globalized version of consumer capitalism. Jean Francois Lyotard believes that the shift is tied to the recognition of difference as the basic reality of life in the face of the collapse of metanarratives that once provided explanation for uniformity and objectivity."[24]

Gilles Deleuze[25] and Felix Guattari[26] suggest that the primary catalyst was the dethroning of reason as the basis for human choice. Michel Foucalt suggests that the unmasking of the Enlightenment notion of objectivity is the key turning point. Jean Baudrillard places the transition within the emergence of an image culture of simulation, where signs have become disconnected from the reality they are supposed to represent.[27] In fact, postmodernism is somewhat a blend of all of the above, but we will now examine some of its primary components. In order to help us remember it's primary features I have presented the information in the form of an acronym: RIPSS.

---

[23] "The objective of this study is the condition of knowledge in the most highly developed societies. I have decided to use the word postmodern to describe that condition. It designates the state of our culture following the 19th century and has altered the game rules for science, literature, and the arts." Jean Francois Lyotard, *The Postmodern Condition* (Minneapolis: Univ. of Minn. Press, reprint 1984), p. viii.

[24] Craig Van Gelder, *Confident Witness-Changing World*, p. 42.

[25] Gilles Deleuze, *The Clamor of Being* (Minneapolis: Univ. of Minn. Press, 1999).

[26] Felix Guattari and Gilles Deleuze, *A Thousand Plateaus* (Minneapolis: Univ. of Minn. Press, 1987).

[27] Craig Van Gelder, *Confident Witness-Changing World*, (Grand Rapids: Eerdmans, 1999), p. 42.

Chapter 2

It's All Relative…Isn't It?

R = Relativity

Postmodernism, as you will see, is not so much a new worldview as it is the disillusionment with the ideals of the Age of Reason. Primarily it is the rejection of rational thinking and the optimism of the modern world. Alister McGrath says,

> "The West has rejected the modernist belief in objective truth, knowable through reason. That rejection can spell trouble, because Christianity has adapted well to the grand vision of the Enlightenment, arguing a reasoned defense against other meta-narratives such as Islam, Marxism, and secularism. Furthermore, as long as Christians were numerically strong and held political and social power, we were seemingly able to make modernism work for us and contribute to the missionary expansion."[28]

---

[28] McGrath, *Evangelicalism and the Future of Christianity*, p. 161.

One of the most elemental tenets of postmodernism is a belief in relativism, which simultaneously dismisses the belief in absolute truth. Thus, since "It's all relative" there can be no one standard…including Christianity. However, the very assertion that there is no absolute truth is, in itself, a self-contradicting claim, because if this claim were true, then there would be at least one absolute truth. Fittingly, we can trace the roots of this concept to a philosopher who was diagnosed with insanity.

Friedrich Nietzsche (1844–1900)

Known primarily for his infamous "God is dead" proclamation, Nietzsche was a forefather of postmodern philosophy. Obviously brilliant, he was appointed professor of classics at Basel University when he was only twenty-four. He suffered from chronic ill health and may very well have been psychosomatic.[29] "He took drugs, argued with almost everyone, wandered Europe in increasing isolation and finally went mad in 1889…His love of Wagner, misogyny, hatred of Christianity and anti-democratic ethics are also well known."[30]

In addition to arguing that God was dead and just a convenience, he also taught that there was no such thing as objective truth because meaning is not a given and we can never get beyond our own perspective. Although he was virtually written off in his own time and was later diagnosed with insanity, today Nietzsche is somewhat of a hero for postmodernists because he publicly introduced most of the ideas that shape current postmodern thought: a worldview empty of God, meaning that is created rather than received, and the concept that what is true depends on who and where you are.

---

[29] F.C. Coplestone, *A History of Philosophy* (New York: Avon Books, 1985), p. 101.

[30] Richard Osborne, *Philosophy for Beginners* (New York: Writers & Readers, 1995), p. 127.

20th century developments in the fields of science and math have also contributed towards the acceptance of relativism. Since the days of Galileo and Newton, Science has always been built upon the belief in a measurable and predictable world, which operates under certain calculable laws. This was the norm until 1905 when Albert Einstein announced his *theory of relativity*. Space and time, he taught, are not absolute, but relative. In certain circumstances, light *could* bend, space *may* slow, and *possibly* even time can slow down. Everything moves, nothing is sure. In an unsettling way Einstein seemed to scientifically confirm the relativism of Nietzsche.[31] In 1920, Werner Heisenberg, an atomic physicist, seemed to add more fuel to the Nietzsche fire. In *his* study of light, he found it impossible to determine the position and speed of subatomic particles which measured in one way showed up as electronic particles, yet measured in another method appeared to be electromagnetic waves. Thus, in the world of quantum physics, you cannot necessarily obtain an objective measure on anything.[32]

Therefore, Heisenberg proposed the "Uncertainty Principle." In simplest terms it states that there is always uncertainty in the simultaneous measurements of the position of a particle.[33] Math, like physics, also used to be taught as a predictable realm in which two plus two always equaled four. Now, we have a new breed of mathematicians, calling themselves chaoticians, who teach a form of math called "chaos theory." This form of

---

[31] It should be noted that, "In science the speed of light in a vacuum is considered an absolute standard. Therefore, scientific relativity does not imply that *all* scientific laws are in a constant state of flux. To use scientific relativity to buttress the concept of relativity in regard to human life and human values is completely invalid." Francis Schaeffer, *The God Who Is There*, p. 141. Interestingly, Einstein almost named it the "theory of invariance" because things are relative to what is invariant or absolute. Douglas Groothuis, *The Death of Truth*, p. 69

[32] Henderson, *Culture Shift*, p. 191.

[33] Richard Appignanesi, *Introducing Postmodernism*, p. 16.

math teaches that some mathematical results may be unpredictable, haphazard, and random. Thus, they conclude that there *may* be some instances when two plus two does *not* equal four.[34]

These relativistic theories have permeated the fields of sociology and religion as well. An individual's belief system is dependant upon who and where you are because truth, like morality, is a relative affair: there are no facts, only interpretations. Ironically, postmodernists have painted themselves into an exclusivist corner by maintaining that all meaning is relative. Conveniently, and under the guise of relativism, they are able to pick and choose an "a la carte" lifestyle from a menu of contradictions.

> Socially, relativistic beliefs are well represented in the ideology of most Gen X-ers. Busters (Generation X) don't believe in absolute truth. To them, everything is relative, and everything *could* be true. They are the first generation to reflect the postmodern ideas circulating in French and American universities since the 1970s. They can live with two contradictory ideas. They can be pro-choice in regard to abortion, for example, and pro-life in regard to whales and trees.[35]

Ironically, "Most relativists really believe that relativism is true for everybody, not just for them. But that is the one thing they cannot hold if

---

[34] Henderson, *Ibid*, p. 191. On a recent short term mission trip to Moscow, one of our team members, Wendy Meredith, encountered such a scenario at Moscow State University, Moscow, Russia in which the student genuinely believed that 2+2 could = 5. (I would have welcomed the opportunity to have done a currency exchange with him.) Often the only methods that seem to work with such postmodern purists is the testimonial and the unlivability argument (see "What about the Matrix theory?" on p. 83).

[35] Dieter Zander, "The Gospel for Generation X" in Marshall Shelley, *Growing Your Church* p. 54.

they are really relativists. So, the relativist who thinks relativism is true for everyone is an absolutist."[36]

In summary of relativism, how much value should anyone seriously give to a theory that has a self-refuting thesis? The postmodernist has thrown the proverbial "baby out with the bathwater" in regards to relativism and truth. The fact that we cannot possess exhaustive truth does not negate the fact that we can know some truth or "true truth". "What kind of world would it be if relativism were true? It would be a world in which nothing is wrong-nothing is considered evil or good, nothing worthy of praise or blame. It would be a world in which justice and fairness are meaningful concepts, in which there would be no accountability, no possibility of moral improvement, no moral discourse."[37]

Relativism is a false and unlivable doctrine. Furthermore, the very fact that it is erroneous means that some moral absolutes do indeed exist. This is a message that, because of its implications, the postmodernist simply doesn't want to hear and yet, as ambassadors of Christ, one that we cannot sidestep. To this relativistic culture that, deep down, is searching for truth, Jesus says, "I am the way, the truth, and the life" (John 14:6). As opportunity presents itself, initiate philosophical and/or spiritual conversations in which you can openly, and in a non-condescending manner, begin to educate your world and culture, one-on-one, on the abysmal foundations of relativistic beliefs.

---

[36] Norman Geisler, *Baker Encyclopedia of Christian Apologetics* (Grand Rapids: Baker, 1999), p. 743.

[37] Francis Beckwith and Gregory Koukl, *Relativism* (Grand Rapids: Baker Books, 1998), p. 69.

Chapter 3

Ignorance Of Christian Beliefs

I = Ignorance

One Sunday night at my church I was asked why we had "three brown letter T's out in front of our church." This woman was referring to the three brown crosses that we use as a symbol of the Christian faith. Just like your spell checker, we can no longer assume that our culture has an understanding of our Christian heritage and terminology. On the Saturday prior to Palm Sunday, our church mobilized some volunteers who canvassed the neighborhoods within a three-mile radius of our church. Our plan was to offer them a complimentary Jesus video with an invitation to join us for a worship service on Easter Sunday. If they were willing, we invited them to participate in ninety second "spiritual background survey."

One of the questions we asked was "What do you know about Scottsdale Bible Church?" To my surprise they knew virtually nothing at all about our church, which was within walking distance of their homes. In fact, the most common response was something like: "you're the big church with the parking problem." On several occasions I tried to explain what SBC was like and our beliefs, but I might as well have been speaking

Greek. As far as they knew we were a Mormon temple. They truly had no idea of terminology that included "evangelical", "non-denominational", etc. Nor did they have the slightest clue as to what the difference was between our "traditional" AM service and our "more contemporary" PM services. They did, however, understand "family friendly", "nursery", and "life applicable spiritual messages".

It has become very obvious that the church needs to rethink its methodologies if it wants to be able to effectively share the Good News with the postmodern. Assumptions that shaped twentieth century thought about our culture's knowledge of Christianity and the Bible are no longer in place. The ignorance in Christian beliefs stems from the fact that the typical postmodernist has not been raised in a Christian home, never attended Vacation Bible School, nor have they ever read the Bible.

The rise in single parent homes, mass immigration, and a general decrease in church attendance in comparison to population growth in the United States have also served to compound the problem. As Francis Schaeffer (in 1968) said, "Thirty or more years ago you could have said things such as 'This is true' or 'That is right' and you would have been on everyone's wavelength."[38] Today, we are even further removed from a shared "wavelength" of reason with the non-Christian culture because they have a very limited and distorted picture of Christianity because few of them have ever been exposed to Christianity from a believer's viewpoint. Rather, the postmodernist exposure to Christian doctrine has been limited to talk show hosts, liberal college professors, and the negative portrayals of Christians in the media and entertainment industry.

In reflection of the above, it should come as no surprise that the number of unchurched adults is rising. The Barna Research Group defines "unchurched" as someone who has not attended a Christian church service during the past six months other than for a wedding, funeral, or holiday service.[39] The number of unchurched Americans increased from 27% in

---

[38] Schaeffer, *The God Who Is There*, p. 27.

1998 to 31% in 1999.[40] "When asked their religious preference, 19% of Gen-Xers responded "none."[41] As Dieter Zander has so accurately pointed out about Generation X: "Perhaps no other generation has needed the church so much, yet sought it so little."[42]

This also helps explain why a traditional favorite like the *Four Spiritual Laws*, for example, sometimes raises more questions than it answers.[43] When telling a postmodernist "God loves you and has a wonderful plan for your life" they very well might sincerely (or sarcastically) reply "God who?" or "Which God?" Secondly, in regards to the fact that God "loves you," they might wonder what exactly is meant by *our* definition of love. The aspect of "has a wonderful plan for your life" may even be interpreted as a rather repressive concept. Furthermore, the appeal of the spiritual laws is futile to the typical postmodern because there are no absolutes or laws within their worldview.

> **People with no religion now account for 14% of the nation.**

Likewise, references to the Bible as an authoritative source is perceived as ludicrous in a world that views it as just another irrelevant meta-narrative. This is not to imply that we cannot or should not use Scripture in gospel presentations. However, we should remember that the postmodernist does not acknowledge the authority or credibility of the Bible and therefore we should be equipped and prepared to defend the authenticity

---

[39] Barna Research Group, *The Barna Report*, Feb. 25, 1999.

[40] George Gallup Jr., *American Spirituality* (Colorado Springs, CO: Cook Publications, 2000), p. 25.

[41] Susan Mitchell, *American Generations* (Ithaca, NY: New Strategist Publications, 1998), p. 75.

[42] Dieter Zander, "The Gospel for Generation X", Marshall Shelley, ed., *Growing Your Church through Evangelism and Outreach* (Nashville: Moorings, 1996), p. 51.

[43] The above analogy is not to be interpreted as a slight against the Four Spiritual Laws, but simply as an illustration to display the genuine ignorance of the postmodern to Christian doctrine.

of the Bible. As a result, we must also be equipped to present the gospel without relying exclusively upon a "Romans Road" type methodology.

An ignorance of Christian beliefs and doctrines means that we cannot presume that a non-believer has an understanding of our beliefs, customs, and terminology. Therefore, like a missionary, we must begin to think of ways in which we can communicate in their language rather than expecting them to take the initiative to learn ours. This can be done by finding appropriate synonyms that translate into postmodernese when discussing spiritual truths.

For example, because of my Baptist background, I used to say that I believed I was a Christian because I had been walked the aisle, been baptized, and attended Vacation Bible School. If you're a Baptist, you know exactly what I'm talking about in reference to "walking an aisle", but if you're a Lutheran or Presbyterian it may not translate. To the postmodernist who is ignorant of Christian beliefs and practices, its even more obscure.

Today when I'm sharing my faith, I simply communicate that I used to believe that I could earn everlasting life through good works. This is something that they can understand and it puts us on the same wavelength. Likewise, I will normally refer to myself as a "follower of Jesus Christ" and I regularly use terms like "Rescuer" and "Forgiver". What about you? Are you using Christianese or postmodernese to communicate to your culture? What would a missionary do? Voltaire said, "If you would speak to me, you must first learn my language." Regarding this quote, listen to Leonard Sweet's observation:

> Coming from a philosopher or from a computer company, these words sound arrogant and elitist. But the church speaks these same words to the culture every Sunday-and every other day of the week, for that matter. The church's language is not even a current one, but an outmoded print language and jungle of jargon that is out of touch with how most people today live and

move and have their being. What if God had refused to dumb down? 'The Word became flesh and his dwelling among us (Jn. 1:14a). This is the essence of the Incarnation-God came to us. God's good ship 'Grace' did not disdain shallow waters[44]

---

[44] Leonard Sweet, *Aqua Church*, p. 167.

Chapter 4

A Pluralistic Conspiracy

P = Pluralism

Don't all religions lead to God? The postmodernist answers this question with a resounding "yes." Regardless of suspect credentials, the postmodern need for political correctness via pluralism and multiculturalism leaves no option but to answer such a question in the affirmative. Although few postmodernists would admit to it, by definition this would even include a Jim Jones type cult because a true pluralist does not believe in any one way of making sense of the world. Rather, pluralism holds that all belief systems are equally true and insists that every culture, and thus its worldview or religion, is equally worthwhile. Since, in their view, everything is a matter of perspective, Christians are considered presumptuous, arrogant and oppressive in teaching Christianity as the *only* true religion. In their eyes, this would be perceived as intolerant and as politically incorrect as asserting the history and literature of Nazi Germany as that most worthy of study.

Since everything is a matter of perspective to the postmodernist, no one has the authority to legislate morality as a result of a particular worldview because we are all equally right. It would be arrogant and judgmental of anyone to insist otherwise. Furthermore, it would be "spiritually racist" for anyone to claim to have the copyright on truth.[45] Besides, to promote Christianity is also perceived as belittling to the non-Christian religions, which is unacceptable in the multicultural society of the new millennium. Therefore, plurality is the only acceptable alternative for the postmodernist.

An article in *Newsweek* entitled "Searching for a Holy Spirit" provides an excellent example of how the postmodern applies plurality:

> In a 1999 poll of teenagers by George Barna, more than half agreed with the statement 'All religious faiths teach equally valid truths.' Where explorers of the baby boom tried on Zen today, Methodism tomorrow, today's teens might cobble together bits of several faiths: a little Buddhist meditation or Roman Catholic ritual, whatever mixture appeals at the time. For example, at the Ramona Convent Secondary School in Los Angeles, Ashling Gabig, 16, receives a traditional diet of Catholic doctrine, yet she has customized her own path of faith. 'My perceptions of God and faith are quite different from those of a devout Catholic,' she says. 'I don't think of the pope as this holy man who is closest to God. I believe in Darwin's theory of evolution, and the possibility of God being a woman. I never believed in the story of Adam and Eve, because it was so demeaning towards women. She does, however, believe in prayer and karma.[46]

---

[45] Rabbi Schmuley Boteach said, "I am absolutely against any religion that says that one faith is superior to another. I don't see how that is anything different than spiritual racism. It's a way of saying that we are closer to God than you, and that leads to hatred." CNN's *Larry King Live* 1/13/2000; Available at http://cnn.com/Transcripts/0001/12/lkl.00.html; Internet.

[46] *Newsweek*, "Searching for the Holy Spirit", May 8, 2000, p. 62.

Similarly, John Hick, who considers himself a liberal Christian pluralist, says, "the fruit of [the] Christian faith seems in general to be neither better nor worse than the fruit of the Jewish, Muslim, Hindu, or Buddhist faiths, should this not lead us to think further about those other great ways?"[47]

In reality, most postmodernists are typically hypocritical when it comes to practicing what they preach regarding political correctness through plurality because tolerance is generally promoted for all faiths with the exception of Christianity. Although, we cannot document this in a "Postmodern Manifesto" it is clearly an unwritten policy within their circles. The intent of postmodern proponents is to dismantle not only modernity, but Christianity as well. Although they preach tolerance, postmodernism has shown no inclination to tolerate any deviation from its own party line. Although they regularly point to examples in the past of how those who believe in absolutes tend to abuse their power and be intolerant of other belief systems; what they haven't shown is that those who deny absolutes *are* not intolerant.

As Bruce Benson states, "Postmodernism is popularly applied to virtually everything which overturns traditional standards. Some of the best known postmodern philosophers are Jacques Derrida, Michael Foucault, Jean-Fracois Lyotard, and Richard Rorty. What unites all these philosophers is their negative response to the modern philosophical paradigm and to the Christianity of modernity."[48] Likewise, "none of the leading postmodern thinkers-whether Rorty, Derrida, Foucalt, Lyotard, or Baudrillard-affirm belief in a personal deity…they deny the objective existence of God and the supernatural".[49]

---

[47] "A Pluralist View" by John Hick in *Four Views of Salvation in a Pluralistic World*, p. 43.
[48] Robert Webber, *Ancient-Future Faith* (Grand Rapids: Baker Books, 1999), p. 22.
[49] Douglas Groothuis, *Truth Decay*, p. 38.

Postmodernists are also very strong advocates for Multiculturalism. On the surface, this, in and of itself, has the potential of being a very valuable component to Christians and non-Christians alike. However, rarely is Christianity or Western Civilization ever included, nor portrayed in a positive manner as other cultures are. Thus, in reality they are hypocritical. This was even demonstrated recently by the disgusting and offensive artwork depicting Jesus in unflattering manners at museums in New York city, whereas nothing short of a riot would have occurred had someone such as Nelson Mandela, Ghandi, Buddha, or Martin Luther King Jr. been substituted in his place. In reality, the postmodern does not promote plurality. Rather, their real focus is limited to the "excluded" cultures and histories. These excluded histories of the "oppressed" typically include Homosexuals, Feminists, Eastern Religions, and Marxists.

Consequently, postmodern activists argue for plurality and advocate the cause of the oppressed by offering *new* versions of "truth."[50] As a result, nearly all American universities, in an effort to be politically correct, now have curricula on and for these "excluded" groups[51] and thus,

---

[50] "Those who want to use the universities, especially the humanities, for leftist political transformation correctly perceive that the Western Rationalistic Tradition is an obstacle in their path...Historically, part of what happened is that in the late 1960s and 1970s a number of young people went into academic life because they thought that the social and political transformation could be achieved through educational and cultural transformation, and that the political ideals of the 1960s could be achieved through education. In many disciplines, for example, analytical philosophy, they found the way blocked by a solid and self-confident professorial establishment committed to traditional intellectual values. But in some disciplines, particularly those humanities disciplines concerned with literary studies-English, French, and Comparative Literature especially-the existing academic norms were fragile, and the way was opened intellectually for a new academic agenda." John R. Searle, "Rationality and Realism, What Is at Stake?" *Daddalus: Proceedings of the American Academy of Arts and Sciences* 122, no. 4 (1993), 70-71.

[51] Dennis McCallum, *The Death of Truth* (Minneapolis: Bethany House Publishers, 1996), p. 49.

we no longer have just "history"; we now have "feminist history" or "gay and lesbian history." Accordingly, in the majority of today's universities, contemporary scholars seek to rearrange information into new paradigms that are politically correct and non-Eurocentric. [52]

> Contemporary scholars seek to dismantle the paradigm of the past and...rewrite history in favor of those who have been excluded from power-women, homosexuals, blacks, Native Americans, and other victims of oppression. Those who celebrate the achievements of Western civilization are accused of narrow-minded Euro-centrism. Patriarchal religions such as Judaism, Islam, and Christianity are challenged and replaced with matriarchal religions; the influence of the Bible is countered by the influence of goddess worship.[53]

The insistence by Christianity for absolute truth is essentially ignored outside of Christian circles. Postmoderns are quick to point out that cultures adhere to different sets of worldviews and therefore accept different authorities. In the postmodern worldview no single reality should be seen as better than another and knowledge or fact is no longer viewed as an end to itself. Rather, knowledge is simply a commodity for those who want power. "Truth becomes the possession of whatever group holds power. When a new group gains power, the truth changes."[54]

The connection between postmodernism and the rejection of fundamentalism may explain in part, why the postmodern avowal of fragmentation and multiplicity tends to attract liberals and radicals. This may be why, in part, feminist theorists have found postmodernism so

---

[52] For an excellent example of the politicizing of college curriculum and campus life activities see *Choosing the Right College: The Whole Truth about America's Top 110 Schools* (Grand Rapids: Eerdman's, 1998).
[53] Robert Veith, *Postmodern Times* (Wheaton: Crossway Books, 1994) p. 57.
[54] Jean Francois Lyotard, *The Postmodern Condition: A Report on Knowledge* (Minneapolis: Univ. of Minnesota Press, reprint, 1984), p. 5

attractive.[55] On another level, however, postmodernism seems to offer some alternatives to joining the global culture of consumption, where commodities and forms of knowledge are offered by forces far beyond any individual's control. These alternatives focus on thinking of any and all action (or social struggle) as necessarily local, limited, and partial-but nonetheless effective.

By discarding "grand narratives" (like the liberation of the entire working class) and focusing on specific local goals (such as improved day care centers for working mothers in your own community), postmodern politics offers a way to theorize local situations as fluid and unpredictable, though influenced by global trends. Consequently, the motto for postmodern politics might well be "think globally, act locally"-and don't worry about any grand scheme or master plan. Christianity seems to bear the brunt of the postmodern anger towards abuse of power via metanarrative. Many of the religion departments in today's typical university even go so far as to portray Christianity as a religion that is oppressive to other people groups. Rather than celebrating his achievements as an explorer, Columbus, for example, is typically portrayed as a Western Christian imperialist who introduced religious oppression to the Americas.[56] In similar fashion, the Crusades of the Middle Ages and the slaughtering of Latin peoples by the Spanish Conquistadors all fall under the umbrella of Christian evangelism in the worldview of the postmodernist.[57] Although,

---

[55] See Sophia Phoca, *Introducing Postfeminism* (New York: Totem Books, 1999).

[56] For an example see Dee Brown's *Bury My Heart at Wounded Knee: An Indian History of the American West* (New York: Bantam Books, 1971), "It all began with Columbus..." p. 1.

[57] To a marginal extent, this is how missions was understood in the Roman Catholic Church: the pagan world outside Europe had to be conquered into the Catholic church. It is also interesting to note that the word mission, in its contemporary sense, was first used in the sixteenth century by Jesuits in Northern Germany to refer to their work of reconverting Protestants to Catholicism. See David Bosch, *Toward a Missiology of Western Culture*, p. 29.

it is true that some of the most heinous crimes in history have been perpetrated under the name of Christianity, they are all in direct and obvious conflict with the message of Jesus and the teachings of the New Testament. Nevertheless, Christians are regularly historically portrayed as narrow-minded, right wing radicals who are devoted to bashing homosexuals, and have no sympathy for women carrying babies they had not planned.

"These new models tend to be adopted without the demands for rigorous evidence required by traditional scholarship. If Euro-centrism is at fault, one would think Afro-centrism would be similarly narrow minded. If patriarchy is wrong, why would matriarchy be any better? But these quibbles miss the point of postmodernist scholarship because truth is not the issue. The issue is power."[58] The attraction of pluralism is not in its claim to truth, but in its claim to promote tolerance. As a result, objectivity is discarded in place of a political correctness that is *not* obligated to be truthful.

> Scholarly debate proceeds not so much by rational argument or the amassing of objective evidence, but by rhetoric (which scheme advances the most progressive ideals?) and by the assertion of power (which scheme advances my particular interest group, or more to the point, which is most likely to win me a research grant, career advancement, and tenure?). Whereas classical scholarship sought the truth, the postmodern academy seeks political correctness. The traditional academic world operated by reason, study, and research; postmodernist academia is governed by ideological agendas, political correctness, and power struggles under the banner of multiculturalism.[59]

---

[58] Veith, *Postmodern Times*, p. 57.
[59] Veith, *Ibid*, p. 58.

True to form, the silence of the postmodernists for people outside of their particular interest groups is absolutely deafening. Case in point would be the Sudan. Since 1983, when a Muslim state was instituted, a holocaust has been taking place akin to Hitler's execution of the Jews that has been absolutely ignored by postmodern politics, scholars and the media. Thus far, over 2.5 million Sudanese have been murdered because of their desire to practice Christianity rather than Islam. Where are the campus protests by the politically correct postmodernists who desire plurality? Where are college professors who denounce the Crusades? As you can see, they conveniently ignore groups that offer no political advancements, grants, or threats of boycotts. Thus, we can conclude that the political correctness and plurality of the postmodernist is somewhat hypocritical.

Chapter 5

Suspicious Minds

S = Skepticism

Ironically, Postmodernism can indirectly trace its lineage to Rene Descartes (1596–1650), a Christian mathematician and philosopher who is often referred to as the "Father of Modern Philosophy." The son of a French councillor in Brittany, Descartes was educated at the Jesuit college of La Fleche where he was impressed by the certainty and precision of mathematics. Descartes is a mixed blessing to both Christian and Postmodern philosophy. On the one hand, he is a rational theist who offers arguments for God's existence and yet his method of calling everything into doubt has served unwittingly and indirectly as a precursor to contemporary postmodern thought.

Although he started out full of skepticism, he was actually seeking and hoping for certainty and so he set out to make a list of the things people could know with absolute certainty. God, the Church, all previous philosophers, and ancient literature were discarded in favor of rational principles from which he could construct a secure system of knowledge. His skepticism began calling everything into question unless he could prove it beyond doubt. His list became shorter and shorter until finally all that he had left was "I think, therefore I am." This became a precursor for a philosophical distrust in anything that was supposed to be obvious or certain. As a result, for Descartes, everything became suspect. "The dualism expressed in Descarte's distinction between *res cognitans* (thinking reality) and *res extensa* (reality extended in space) created a state in which it was necessarily doubtful whether the gap between these two worlds could be bridged. A skepticism about whether our senses give us access to reality became the background for most philosophical thinking ever since."[60]

In the 20th century, Jean Francois Lyotard, author of *The Postmodern Condition: A Report on Knowledge*, would put a different spin on skepticism in order to express a general distrust in any ideology. According to Lyotard, metanarratives are the theoretical worldviews that are used to legitimize and manipulate various projects, religious, political or scientific. Examples are: the emancipation of humanity through that of the workers (Marx); the creation of wealth (Adam Smith); Christianity (Jesus); the evolution of life (Darwin); the dominance of the unconscious mind (Freud), etc.[61] In short, Lyotard defined postmodernism as "incredulity toward metanarratives."[62]

According to his theory, the way that modern societies went about creating categories labeled as "order" or "disorder" have to do with the effort to achieve stability. Lyotard equated that stability with the idea of "totality," or a totalized system.[63] Totality, stability, and social order, Lyotard argued, are maintained in modern societies through the means of "grand

---

[60] Lesslie Newbigin, *The Gospel in a Pluralistic Society* (Grand Rapids: Wm. B. Eerdmans, 1989), p. 18.

[61] Powell, *Postmodernism for Beginners*, p. 29.

[62] Jean Francois Lyotard, *The Postmodern Condition*, (Minneapolis: U. of Minnesota Press, 1966), p. 10.

[63] Jean Francois Lyotard, *The Postmodern Explained* (Minneapolis: U. of Minnesota Press, 1992), pp. 55-59.

narratives" or "master narratives," which are stories a culture tells itself about its practices and beliefs. A "grand narrative" in American culture, for example, might be the story that democracy is the most enlightened (rational) form of government, and that it provides the best opportunity for human happiness and prosperity. According to Lyotard, every belief system or ideology has its grand narratives

Modernity was fundamentally about rationality and creating order out of chaos. The assumption was that creating more rationality is conducive to creating more order, and that the more ordered a society is, the better it will function (the more rationally it will function). The postmodernist believes that because modernity was about the pursuit of ever-increasing levels of order, modern societies constantly are on guard against anything and everything labeled as "disorder," which might disrupt order. Thus, they propose that modern societies rely on the establishment of a metanarrative by simultaneously establishing an anti-metanarrative in order that they can assert the superiority of their metanarrative. According to the postmodernist, this is includes Christianity and therefore anything non-white, non-male, non-heterosexual, non-rational, and non-Christian becomes part of the anti-metanarrative, and has to be eliminated from the ordered, rational modern society.

Lyotard proposes that all aspects of modern societies (including science) depend on these grand narratives. [64] Those influenced by these aspects of postmodernism then are naturally suspicious of grand narratives because any attempt to create order always demands the creation of an equal amount of disorder, which results in oppression.

---

[64] Jean Francois Lyotard, *The Postmodern Condition*, p. 25. The postmodern attack on science is represented in the writings of Vine Deloria who says, "Science should drop the pretense of having absolute authority with regard to human origins and begin looking for some other kind of explanation that would include the traditions of non-Western peoples." *Red Earth, White Lies* (Golden, CO: Fulcrum, 1997), p. 5.

This theme is closely related to triumphalism; a dirty word in postmodern societies and one that they accuse Christians of being guilty of. Tim Burton perhaps illustrated this sentiment in his 2001 version of *Planet of the Apes* in which he illustrated that whoever controls the religious beliefs also gets to control the society.

Postmodernism, in rejecting grand narratives, favors mini-narratives, stories that explain small practices, local events, rather than large-scale universal or global concepts such as Christianity. Postmodern mini-narratives are always situational, conditional, contingent, and temporary, making no claim to universality, truth, reason, or stability. Christianity is simply seen as another metanarrative that, like others, ignorantly claims to be able to give an account for the origins of life and creation. Only Fundamentalists (e.g. Christians) are arrogant enough to insist that theirs is superior to the metanarratives or mini-narratives of others. (Postmodernists label fundamentalists as unacceptable because they subscribe to universal truth claims). Those who believe in universal explanations for reality are considered to be totalistic or "logocentric" which, to the postmodernist, is a great atrocity. [65] "Logocentrists are the ideologues, the cultural imperialists who attempt to subjugate others to their version of the truth."[66] Rather, postmodernists believe that each group tells its own story or narrative, and that these beliefs should never discount,

---

[65] Logocentrism desires a perfectly rational language that represents the real world. Such a language of reason would absolutely guarantee that the very presence of the world and the essence of everything in the world could be transparently presented to an observing subject who could speak of it with complete certainty. Jacques Derrida taught that reason is a tyranny and a "white male construct" which can only be sustained by the evils of repressing or excluding what is uncertain or different. To postmodernists, the atrocities committed by rationalistic Western cultures (Hiroshima, Auschwitz, etc) is evidence that Logocentrism is ludicrous and even dangerous because all meaning is provisional and relative, but never exhaustive. [*Introducing Postmodernism*, p. 78-79].

[66] McCallum, *The Death of Truth*, p. 91.

exclude, or marginalize.[67] This explains some of their misdirected hostility towards Christianity.

> [To] people of liberal political convictions, the multicultural agenda demands that religions not be permitted to make truth claims, in order to avoid triumphalism or imperialism. Indeed, there seems to be a widespread perception that the rejection of religious pluralism entails intolerance or unacceptable claims to exclusivity. In effect, the liberal political agenda dictates that all religions should be treated on an equal footing. But is there any reason for progressing from the acceptable demand that we should respect religions other than our own, to the more radical demand that we regard them all as the same or as equally valid routes to a common salvation?[68]

However, the primary problem with this concept is yet another violation of the Law of Non-Contradiction. As Ravi Zacharias says, "If truth does not exclude, then no assertion of a truth claim is being made; just an opinion that is being stated. Any time you make a truth claim, you mean something contrary to it is false. Truth excludes its opposite…to deny the exclusive nature of truth is to make a truth claim, and is not that person not arrogant too? That's the boomerang effect that the condemner often doesn't pause to consider."[69]

---

[67] McCallum, *Ibid*, p. 201.
[68] Dennis Okholm, *Four View of Salvation in a Pluralistic World*, quoting Alister McGrath, p. 151.
[69] Lee Strobel, *The Case for Faith* (Grand Rapids: Zondervan, 2000), p. 210.

Chapter 6

Spiritual Curiousity

S = Spiritually Curious

Nietzsche was off…way off. Not only is God not dead, he's big business. Just walk into any of your favorite secular bookstores and take a look at the number of books that are focused on spirituality. The typical secular bookstore has entire sections devoted to spirituality, new age, wicca, Eastern thought, Judaism, Islam, and, yes, even Christianity. In the summer of 2002 I was pleasantly surprised that during a recent trip to one of my favorite secular bookstores that the very first book I saw as I walked through the doors was one of the most recent volumes in Tim LaHaye's *Left Behind* series. However, on the very same table was *Harry Potter*. The spiritual curiosity of the Postmodern is clearly reflected in the fact that both *The Prayer of Jabez* and *Harry Potter* can share the best seller list.

> We see it all around us. From cover stories of national news magazines, to titles of best-selling books, to themes of television programs and movies, to songs on the music charts-people are hungry for information about God. Spiritual interest is at a high

> level in our culture but so is bewilderment about what to believe and whom to trust. The good news is that although there is growing suspicion of organized religion, many men and women are still willing to turn to an ordinary church like yours or mine in the hope that they might-just might-find answers there. The issue is whether or not we are prepared to help them.[70]

In 1990 John Naisbett accurately forecasted that the late nineties and early 21st century would experience an increased and renewed interest in spirituality, but that they would not necessarily seek out the mainline Christian denominations to have these needs met.[71] He was right. The late Twentieth century experienced a remarkable revival of the "Old Religions" and many groups identify with Celtic, Egyptian, Wicca, Goddess, and Native American traditions. (Even the trail of those interested in the UFO phenomenon often leads to the occult or a New Age practice).

> Angels are all over the place these days. Occult practices have become very prominent. Folk magic and astrology pervade our context, and not just among the socially marginal communities where such beliefs have always existed as a type of subculture. Such beliefs are popular even among the cultural elites. It is not unusual these days to find university professors who practice pre-Christian goddess religions, therapists who employ shamanic techniques, or computer programmers who consult their astrological charts. Practices of this sort make it important for us to reevaluate our situation: ours is a missionary location.[72]

---

[70] Mittelberg, *Building a Contagious Church*, p. 19.
[71] John Naisbitt, *Megatrends 2000* (New York: Avon Books, 1990), p. 290.
[72] Richard J. Mouw, "The Missionary Location of the North American Churches" in Craig Van Gelder, *Confident Witness-Changing World*, (Grand Rapids: Eerdmans Publishing, 1999), p. 4.

The interest in spirituality by Americans is well documented in George Gallup's *The Next American Spirituality*:

> As we enter a new millennium, religious belief seems poised to thrive and flourish. "Religion makes a comeback,: declared a New York Times Magazine lead story. "America has outgrown its 'take it or leave it' attitude toward religion," the article continued. "Now, even people without faith are looking for God." The article led with a sentence that seems hardly at home in the urbane newspaper: "Is America in the grip of a religious revival?"[73]

An August 2000 poll by Gallup revealed that 85% of Gen-X respondents said religion was important to them personally and that religion could solve the world's problems.

Although the "revival" is in spirituality and not in Christianity per se, the church should recognize it's unique position in being the only eligible candidate to truly meet this need and equip its' members to translate the gospel into a vernacular that the spiritually curious postmodernist can understand. We must also begin to think of new vehicles in which we can introduce spiritual truths to a spiritually curious and spiritually hungry generation. (We will examine this in part three).

---

[73] George Gallup, Jr., *The Next American Spirituality* (Colorado Springs: Cook Communications, 2000, p. 26, citing Jack Miles, "Religion Makes A Comeback," *New York Times Magazine*, December 12, 1997.

Part II
Postmodern Entertainment

"What we have here is a failure to communicate."
—Cool Hand Luke (Paul Newman) in *Cool Hand Luke*

Chapter 7

Popcorn & Postmodernism

Big & Small Screen

Postmodern ideologies are becoming articulated on a more regular basis within the entertainment industry. Descriptive of 21st century America, entertainment is one of the most influential mediums for representing a unique type of language that has the ability to reflect our most essential cultural beliefs. Some of the trendiest new musical artists, such as Radiohead, unknowingly reflect postmodern thought in their intentionally nonsensical and confusing lyrics that incorporate a plurality of styles.[74]

Whereas, just fifty years ago, books were a typical conversational topic, television and movies have been substituted in their place in the post-literate

---

[74] *Radiohead* is presently one of the more popular British alternative music groups that recently won a Grammy. There has been such an increase in blended styles such as techno and jazz, folk and punk, etc. that many music stores are perplexed at how to correctly label and categorize the latest groups and styles.

culture.[75] A study conducted by William Costanzo discovered that the typical American college student watches an average of twenty-two movies a month, a figure that has grown substantially with the rise of cable TV and VCRs.[76] A development in entertainment that began to show up in film in the late 1960s was a transition towards plots that explored the character's psychological state. "Characters are often confused, ambivalent, alienated; their goals and desires uncertain; and their actions inconsistent and often followed by self-doubt."[77] This development includes shifts within the content of movie narratives, differences of approach and perspective by various directors, developments in the technology of movie making, and continued changes in the general cultural milieu. It is the very malleability of movies that has made them such a natural medium for expressing the postmodern condition.[78]

This trend in entertainment is identified with a perspective that comes from viewing topics from multiple viewpoints, which consist of truth claims that depend on the angle of one's outlook. In entertainment it is the truth or perspective of the director or producer that is presented. Authenticity and validity are optional. *Blue Velvet* is considered by many to be the "quintessential postmodern movie."[79] It introduces the viewer to a collage of postmodern themes, such as combining past and present, fantasy and exploitation, violence without moral direction or judgment, the power of gazing/viewing in shaping the voyeur's identity, and exposing the

---

[75] For an excellent analysis and for further reading see Neil Postman's *Amusing Ourselves to Death*.

[76] William Costanzo, *Reading the Movies* (Urbana, Ill: National Council of Teachers, 1992), p.51.

[77] William Romanowski, *Pop Culture Wars: Religion & the Role of Entertainment in American Life* (Downers Grove: InterVarsity Press, 1996), p. 232.

[78] Craig Van Gelder, "Reading Postmodern Culture through the Medium of Movies" in *Confident Witness-Changing World*, 1999, p. 51.

[79] Norman Denzin, *Images of Postmodern Society* (Newberry Park, CA: Sage Publications, 1991), p. viii

darker side within the best of any human motive. Jeffery, the main character, is able to cross into and out of a peaceful, suburban existence with Sandy as if the other world did not exist. "The movie's postmodern subversion is to invite (force) the viewer to explore (own) the realities of his/her own darker side."[80]

Movies such as Bladerunner[81], Contact, Matrix, Planet of the Apes (2001) and television programs such as Charmed, Crossing Over, Sabrina, Buffy the Vampire Slayer, X-Files, Enterprise and Star Trek: The Next Generation[82] also reflect postmodern themes. In the Matrix, one of the main characters, Neo, has hidden several secret computer discs in a hollowed copy of Jean Baudrillard's (a French Postmodern philosopher) *Simulacra and Simulation* in which the author's thesis challenges us to question whether we can truly ever know what is real and authentic. Oprah Winfrey, perhaps the most influential culture shaper on television provides a heavy spiritual diet of New Age and Eastern spirituality via guests such as Gary Zukav, Caroline Myss, Marianne Williamson, and Iyanla Vanzant.

Not to be outdone by talk shows targeted towards women viewers, children are now raised on a postmodern diet through comic books. A series in *Wonder Woman* entitled "War of the Gods"[83] clearly reflected pluralism and the newest version of the *Spectre*[84] is perhaps the most spiritual and postmodernly philosophical comic book ever produced. Whereas in the past the goal of a comic book super hero was simply to fight against evil,

---

[80] Craig Van Gelder, *Confident Witness-Changing World*, p. 57.

[81] Due to its' fragmentary nature and use of simulacrum *Bladerunner* is considered by some to be the first movie to intentionally develop postmodern themes. See "Postmodern Artifacts" in *Postmodernism for Beginners*, pp. 122-129.

[82] For an excellent analysis of *Star Trek the Next Generation* see chapter one "Star Trek and the Postmodern Generation" in Stanley Grenz's *A Primer on Postmodernism* (Grand Rapids: Eerdmans, 1996).

[83] *Wonder Woman*, "War of the Gods," Sept-Nov, 2000, DC Comics, New York,

[84] *Spectre*, DC Comics, New York, 2001. See especially issues 1-7, March-Sept 2001.

the Spectre struggles with the very concept of what exactly evil is, as well as how it should be classified, and how to fight it.

Although The *Matrix* may be the best recent example of a postmodern movie due to its Baudrillardian portrayal of simulacra, Tim Burton's 2001 version of *Planet of the Apes*, in my opinion, is the "quintessential" postmodern movie. This is because Burton is able to demonstrate the misuse of religious beliefs for oppression and control. Likewise, he clearly demonstrates that the beliefs do not have to be authentic or valid in order for it to be used as a vehicle to wield control.

Oliver Stone is another great example of postmodern entertainment in that he is able to present relativism through the multiple conspiracy theories for the assassination of John F. Kennedy in *JFK* that are essentially all based on the same original primary sources: eye-witness accounts, written testimonies, audio tapes, and video tapes and yet each develops his own interpretation of the events. "Because of the historical character of the event of the assassination, and the representative power of film to present images that appear to portray history, *JFK* took on a life of its own. In it Stone demonstrates the power of the medium of film to construct alternative meanings."[85] In *Nixon* and *Natural Born Killers*, Stone continues to develop the theme that reality and truth are often not what they appear, and in fact, may be the very opposite.

Those influenced by the Modern period produced very typical movie narratives with clear story lines and predictable characters. Ambivalence, inconsistency, and irrationality in entertainment is not the result of exceptional creativity by contemporary writers. Rather, in my opinion, it is simply a reflection of a postmodern culture.

---

[85] Craig Van Gelder, *Ibid*, p. 59.

Chapter 8

Postmodern Art

Art provides a very intriguing overview of worldview development. David Henderson provides an example of how art reflects the different stages of worldview development from his visit to the National Art Gallery in Washington, D.C. Due to the fact that he was pressed for time he decided to tour the gallery by starting at the end, which provided a chronological order beginning with the Middle Ages and ending with the Postmodern.

The premodern art era naturally reflects a worldview with God at the center which is represented by the fact that God, Jesus, angels, John the Baptist, and Mary are the predominant focus of the various artists of this period.

> As you move into the Renaissance section you begin to notice a change. Nature and humanity come to the fore, with the Bible stories and the ancient legends of the gods serving as mere backdrops. By the time you reach the Romantic period, Man looms large. When you pass from the Romantics through the Impressionist into 'modern' art, the next change is obvious. We jump from Cecil B. DeMille to MTV. Modern art abandons the real world. In rapid succession, the works lose the grand themes,

lose focus, lose resemblance to real life, lose a single point of perspective, and ultimately lose coherence. Chaotic, broken, and dark, they evoke and provoke, teasing the eye, taunting the mind, tearing at the heart. Postmodernism ushered in a world that hums with the supernatural but is absent of God, is filled with opportunity but lacks any inherent meaning.[86]

Another excellent example of the ethos in postmodern art is represented by Dadaism.[87] Dadaism arose in nihilist protest to the vast mechanized assembly-line slaughter of World War One-the last war to ever be fought between imperial dynasties and the first to exploit modern technology-machine guns, poison gas, tanks, and airplanes. This art form ignored all the traditional rules of art in favor of chance as the primary methodology. Dada is a chance concept. The artist Jackson Pollock (1912–1956), for example, put his canvases on the floor and dripped paint on them by chance. After doing this for some time he felt he had exhausted the chance method. This left him no way to go on further, which may have contributed towards his suicide. Francis Schaeffer said:

> "In the same way (by chance) they composed their poems. They cut printed words out of the newspaper, threw them in a hat, and picked them out by chance. But these men were deadly serious; it really was no game they were playing...there is always a nonsense element. What are they saying? Everything is chance. Chance, the nothingness, is not just shut up in a framed picture, but it is the structure of life. You are in the chance, in the nothingness. You are the destroyed ones."[88]

---

[86] Henderson, *Culture Shift*. p. 187-188.

[87] The term Dadaism was determined by chance. One day several artists flipped through a French dictionary in Zurich in the Café Voltaire. They put a finger down at random and found that it rested on the word *dada*. Therefore, they appropriately conceived the name for this form of art by chance.

[88] Francis Schaeffer, *The God Who Is There*, pp. 52-53.

Leonard Sweet has astutely described the postmodern culture as being "visualholic" due to its dependence on images and metaphors for communication.[89] Therefore, based upon some of the more recent trends in art, we may surmise that not only are postmoderns ignorant regarding Christian beliefs and doctrines, but that many are also hostile towards Christianity in general. One of the common denominators that they seem to rally around is their general disdain for Christians or morally based metanarratives. It is a culture that embraces Madonna while being openly hostile towards the common sense morals of a Laura Schlessinger. Indeed we are in a similar cultural boat as our first century predecessors. Likewise, many, given the opportunity, would feed us to the lions. May we boldly rise to the occasion as our spiritual predecessors did.

---

[89] Leonard Sweet, *Postmodern Pilgrims* (Nashville: Broadman & Holman, 2000), p. 92.

Part III
Prerequisites For Postmodern Ministry

"I cant believe your fickleness-how easily you have turned traitor to him who called you by the grace of Christ by embracing a variant message! It is not a minor variation, you know; it is completely other, an alien message, a no-message, a lie about God. Those who are provoking this agitation among you are turning the Message of Christ on its head. Let me be blunt: If one of us-even if an angel from heaven!-were to preach something other than what we preached originally, let him be cursed. I said it once; I'll say it again: If anyone, regardless of reputation or credentials, preaches something other than what you received originally, let him be cursed. Do you think I speak this strongly in order to manipulate crowds? Or curry favor with God? Or get popular applause? If my goal was popularity, I wouldn't bother being Christ's slave. Know this-I am most emphatic here, friends-this great Message I delivered to you is not mere human optimism. I didn't receive it through the traditions, and I wasn't taught it in some school. I got it straight from God, received the Message directly from Jesus Christ."

—Paul the Apostle, Galatians 1: 6–12, *The Message*

Chapter 9

No Compromise

During the Enlightenment many in the church decided to enfold the Age of Reason. Many seminaries became embarrassed at biblical references to miracles, angels, and anything supernatural because they were not within the new pale of Enlightenment orthodoxy. For the Age of Reason, anything supernatural was grouped into the same category as ghosts, werewolves, and fairies. So, in spite of revelation to the contrary, many seminaries abandoned their beliefs in the supernatural. The supernatural aspects of Christianity were abandoned due to cultural and intellectual peer pressure.[90] The repercussions of this shift within the seminaries[91]

---

[90] One of the most prominent thinkers of this era, Thomas Jefferson, provides us with an example of the Enlightenment's influence. Although he was a great lover of books, Jefferson himself only wrote two, one of which was the *Jefferson Bible*. For its composition, he took the Gospels and with a pair of scissors cut out all of the supernatural and miraculous contents, yet keeping the moral teachings of Christ intact. He honestly believed in the moral teachings of Jesus, which he deemed to be "the most sublime and benevolent code of morals which has ever been offered to man."

[91] In 1825 the American Unitarian Association was formed, which was composed predominantly of Deists. "Harvard Divinity School became its official seminary." *The Story of Christian Theology*, p. 532.

soon found its way into churches throughout America as many ecclesiastical leaders also became uncomfortable with the supernatural elements of Christianity. Eventually these churches, and in some cases entire denominations, unwittingly found themselves on the slippery slope of theological compromise in order to remain *contemporary*.

Based on church history it is rather safe to say that attempting to make Christian *doctrine* more palatable and "user-friendly" in order to be in sync with culture, trends, and pop philosophy is a path that ultimately leads to demise. Historically, culture has never been a very reliable source. For example, there was a time when it was culturally acceptable to own slaves and to prohibit women from voting in the United States. Today, very few educated people in the United States would argue for such practices and even consider them immoral. Thus, if it is risky for the secular world to rely upon cultural acceptability, the church should be even more circumspect about where its influence comes from.

Adapting theology to fit cultural trends cannot only become heretical but it also results in a loss of influence upon the culture. Liberal churches, for example, have failed to gain the acceptance of the culture that they change for.

> "Liberal and neo-orthodox influenced denominations have experienced a steady and accelerating decline in attendance as the culture they sought to appease and initiate rejected them. The liberal leaders failed to notice that a church without the supernatural God of the Bible had nothing to offer a lost culture. In fact, many parishioners left the "liberal" churches by the droves, whereas fundamental evangelicalism experienced growth during the same period. By contrast, the evangelical churches that refused to compromise morality or truth never experienced the same losses. In fact, they continued to grow even during the 1960s, 70s, and 80s."[92]

---

[92] *Ibid*, p. 236.

Therefore, the postmodern era church must be wary of allowing itself to compromise orthodox theology in order to be en vogue with the culture it seeks to evangelize.

From its conception, Christianity has been culturally unacceptable. "The Christian proclamation has always taken place in a pluralistic world, in competition with rival religious and intellectual convictions. The emergence of the gospel within the matrix of Judaism, the expansion of the gospel in a Hellenistic milieu, the early Christian expansion in pagan Rome, the establishment of the Mar Thoma church in southeastern India demonstrates how the church has and will flourish in virtually any environment."[93]

The pre-Constantinian Roman Empire was, to say the least, a pluralistic society.

Though they had lost their ancient virtues, Romans were supremely tolerant. Like postmodernists today, the only people they could not tolerate were the Christians. During the persecutions Christians who refused to recant their faith had their legal rights suspended and could be instantly put to death-under a legal system otherwise scrupulously fair.[94] Historian Stephen Benko has noted that the primary reason Christians were so brutally persecuted was because they claimed to possess exclusive truth. The Christians refusal to acknowledge the deity of the Emperor was cause enough for persecution but what really irked them was the fact that these "low-life presumptive slaves claimed to possess the *only* truth."[95]

"The church, however, did not try to conform to the pattern of the world. It refused to compromise its principles. Far from being popular and

---

[93] Alister McGrath, *Evangelicalism & the Future of Christianity* (Downer's Grove: Intervarsity Press, 1995), p. 162.
[94] Veith, *Postmodern Times*, p. 229
[95] Stephen Benko, *Pagan Rome and the Early Chrisians* (Bloomington: Indiana Univ. Press, 1984), p. 58.

socially acceptable, Christianity was despised. Evangelism efforts were complicated by the fact that those who became Christians faced the death penalty. (Now there's a problem in church marketing.) Thousands of Christians were martyred. Nevertheless, the Holy Spirit kept bringing people to Christ."[96]

Robert Webber, professor of theology at Wheaton College says, "Some church leaders will insist on preserving the Christian faith in its modern form; others will run headlong into the sweeping changes that accommodate Christianity to postmodern forms; and a third group will carefully and cautiously seek to interface historic Christian truths into the dawning of a new era."[97] It is within the third camp that we should aspire to be in. In an attempt to make Christianity more palatable factions within the church have veered off course whereas those who have remained true to orthodox Christian doctrine, in spite of intense peer pressure to do otherwise, have thrived. It was during the Enlightenment that the "Methodist movement in the English-speaking world and the Pietist movement within Lutheranism countered Enlightenment rationalism with a supernatural, emotional spirituality. In America, the Age of Reason was accompanied by the Great Awakening."[98] The emergence of Liberalism inadvertently created the rise of Fundamentalism in early 20th century America. The challenge for today's local church is to evangelize the postmodern culture while remaining true to orthodox Christian doctrine.

As Dennis McCallum said:

> "Standing for the truth often appears risky to the natural mind, and even to the converted mind. When the truth directly opposes beloved convictions held by the majority of our contemporaries, only the courageous dare speak it. But we, as Christians, are to minister with the power of God. We find our

---

[96] Veith, *Postmodern Times*, p. 230.
[97] Robert Webber, *Ancient-Future Faith* (Grand Rapids: Baker Books, 1999), p. 14.
[98] Veith, *Postmodern Times*, p. 230.

faithfulness challenged when the Word of God tells us something we know might offend our culture. But the alternative is even worse: becoming cultural prostitutes, prepared to jettison God's revealed truth for the sake of imagined popularity. When we take this course, we lose any voice we might have had. Our imagined new friends from the academic world and popular culture will never love us anyway, and the power of the Spirit of God will be quenched pitifully."[99]

Postmodernism in the Pews

It is not a surprise that in North America, Christianity it now seen as one of the many possible ways to God. Nor, should it be shocking that the exclusive nature of traditional Christian doctrine regarding salvation is condemned as spiritually racist, logocentric, politically incorrect and even arrogant. As Dennis Okholm said, "In our politically correct environment, exclusivism is akin to flapping a red flag before a bull."[100] This is to be expected in a postmodern culture that celebrates multiculturalism and the exaltation of marginalized and non-Western beliefs. It is also well represented within the media whenever religious issues are addressed. However, it is disturbing to witness these same pressures from *within* the Body of Christ especially when they are in stark contrast to the teachings of Jesus Christ.

Some theologians seem to celebrate the end of the exclusiveness of Christianity and welcome pluralistic ideologies into the fold of Christianity with open arms. However, these views have not arisen through theological or biblical studies. Rather, they are sociologically

---

[99] *Ibid*, p. 237.
[100] Dennis Okholm & Timothy Phillips, editors, *4 Views of Salvation in a Pluralistic World*, (Grand Rapids: Zondervan, 1996) p. 15.

inspired. Evangelical Christianity will continually be pressured to discard the exclusivity of salvation through Jesus Christ in favor of a more politically correct and tolerant stance, which incorporates pluralism or inclusivism. As a result, the exclusivist view will continually be portrayed by the more liberal scholars, such as John Hick and John Dominic Crossan (Jesus Seminar), as the view that is reserved for fundamentalists who are far removed from mainstream culture and Christianity. In a response to the exclusivist view presented by R. Douglas Geivett and W. Gary Phillips in *Four Views of Salvation in a Pluralistic World*, John Hick said,

> "...there is a vast gap between Geivett/Phillips' use of the texts and that which they would find in such acknowledged centers of scholar ship as Harvard, Yale, Chicago, Princeton, Vanderbilt, Duke, and Claremont. For example, Geivett/Phillips speak of 'Jesus Christ, who both claimed to be God and corroborated his claim by rising from the dead.' Even New Testament scholars, who are personally orthodox in their beliefs, are agreed today that Jesus did not teach that he was God...The most recent major lives of Jesus-John Dominic Crossan's *The Historical Jesus* (1991) and *Jesus* (1994), and E.P. Sanders' *The Historical Figure of Jesus* (1993)—do not support the Geivett/Phillips picture of Jesus at all."[101]

Although a vast majority of scholars acknowledge that Jesus did regard himself as God, we should anticipate that due to their political correctness, it will be the views of Hick and Crossan that will become the spokesmen for Christianity within the media. If the pluralistic teachings of John Hick and inclusivist views of Clark Pinnock are considered *evangelical* then perhaps, once again, those of us who believe in the authority and inspiration of Scripture need to adopt a new label.

---

[101] *Ibid*, John Hick in "Response to Geivett and Phillips," p. 249.

Salvation outside of Jesus Christ is simply not seen nor taught in the New Testament and as far as the writers of the New Testament are concerned, salvation is dependant upon a personal faith in Jesus Christ. When asked by the Gentile jailer what he must do to be saved, Paul and Silas replied: "Believe in the Lord Jesus, and you shall be saved" (Acts 16:30–31). "If salvation could come apart from knowledge about Jesus, Paul and Silas seem confidently oblivious of that option."[102] Likewise, the devout and religious Nicodemus, a man who was well versed in the Scriptures, was instructed by Jesus, "You should not be surprised at my saying, 'You must be born again" (John 3:7 NIV). No other mode for salvation is ever referenced.

Thus, any arguments for other modes of salvation, including through general revelation or inclusivism, is one that must be argued for on grounds of logic, philosophy, or political correctness, but it simply cannot be supported via the NT.[103] In fact, the NT teaches a very Christocentric mode of salvation. "There is salvation in no one else, for there is no other *name* under heaven given among mortal men by which we must be saved" (Acts 4:12 emphasis mine). "Peter uses the broad phrase 'under heaven' to indicate how extensive his exclusion of all other names actually is…Although the particularist should not rest his case of this verse alone, it does imply that the requirement of salvation by belief in Jesus' name is universal."[104] This is consistent with Christ's teachings regarding salvation in John (14:6) and in his analogy of the "narrow gate" (Mt 7:13,14).[105]

---

[102] *Ibid*, Geivett and Phillips, "A Particularist View" in *Four Views of Salvation*, p.231.

[103] Although Romans (1:21) indicates that general revelation is sufficient for condemnation there is no suggestion or implication that it is sufficient for redemption.

[104] Geivett and Phillips in *Four Views of Salvation*, p. 230.

[105] In the parallel passage in Luke 13:24, the *Nelson Study Bible* commentators say, "The suggestion here is that one must enter salvation on God's terms. Those that seek to enter but are unable are those who seek entrance on their own terms. Many will miss the blessings of God because they think they can achieve salvation on their own merit or on the basis of their own piety, rather than because they came to know God through Jesus."

There are many debatable and negotiable topics within evangelical Christianity in which there can be disagreement without heresy. However, the doctrine of salvation is not one of them. It is a non-negotiable. It is a fundamental tenet of orthodox and classic Christianity, which cannot be compromised regardless of its unpopularity. Simply put, it is an *essential* of Christian doctrine. To compromise on this doctrine is the equivalent of apostasy and we should revisit the classification of such proponents, regardless of title, degree, or position as an evangelical if they propose another gospel. The pressure to conform to a pluralistic and politically correct gospel will continue to gain momentum, but it is essential that we maintain our exclusivist gospel in order to remain true to the Scriptures and to be able to offer a valid and legitimate hope to our postmodern culture.

> "We have a mandate to please God alone by preaching the pure gospel message alone-whether people like it or not. The ironic thing is that most real seekers are looking for a leader who has the courage to look them in the eye and tell them the truth about their spiritual predicament-and then show them the way to the One who can help. And even when people don't want to hear about the cross-and some truly won't, as the Bible predicts-we need to preach Christ anyway, asking him to use our efforts, bless his message, and draw people to himself."[106]

Paul provided a very stern warning to the church in Galatia regarding any alteration of the Gospel:

> "But even though we, or an angel from heaven, should preach to you a gospel contrary to that which we have preached to you, let him be accursed. As we have said before, so I say again now, if any man is preaching to you a gospel contrary to that which you have received let him be accursed. For am I now seeking the

---

[106] Mittelberg, *Building A Contagious Church*, p. 346.

favor of men, or of God? Or am I striving to please men? If I were still trying to please men, I would not be a bond-servant of Christ" (Galatians 1:8–10).

Regardless of political and sociological pressure to compromise, we must stand firm.

Chapter 10

Intentional Evangelism

Lack of focus is probably the single greatest problem in most churches today. According to Bill Hull: "Too many pastors and church leaders plant their philosophical feet firmly in the air; that is, they do not possess a solid, functional theology of mission for the church. The importance of a theology of mission cannot be overstated."[107] Not very long ago it was assumed by most that the church was one of the central institutions in Western culture. The physical location of churches in the center of most American cities and towns in the 18th and 19th centuries testifies to this influential role. Likewise, the pastor was automatically considered a community leader.[108] There was a widely shared agreement even among non-churchgoers that "Christian values" were the basis of Western civilization. However, the cultural centrality of the church has been undergoing a radical transformation for more than a century—especially since the early 1970s. It is very evident that we no longer live in a Christian culture.

---

[107] Bill Hull, *Can We Save the Evangelical Church?* (Grand Rapids: Revell, 1993), p. 29.
[108] See David Wells, *No Place for Truth*. Chapter 1 – "A Delicious Paradise Lost" (Grand Rapids: Eerdmans, 1993).

Indeed postmodernity has drastically undermined a view of culture in which religious faith in general and Christian belief in particular provided the unifying bonds for a coherent worldview. Today, given the pervasiveness of pluralism and the accompanying ethnic and social diversity, this is no longer credible for many people. In fact, no single voice or entity can claim to speak for everyone today. As a result, many traditional churches are under attack, including the institutional church.[109]

Surprisingly, most churches are still investing their time and energy into ministry, worship, and evangelism methodologies that were developed in and for the modern era. They continue to assume that what worked in the 1950s will work now, if we just try a little harder. Other churches have noticed the culture shift and are scrambling to do something about it. However, evangelizing postmoderns is more than just singing praise choruses in place of hymns, using PowerPoint slides for sermon delivery, and dressing casual. It's also more than just thinking of evangelism as a program or product. This is about the church adopting a missional ethos that will necessitate updated training in personal evangelism for the local church to effectively reach its community.

In 1990, Kenneth Callhoun accurately noted that the "day of the churched-culture local church is over and the local church needs to begin seeing itself as a 'mission outpost.'"[110] The 21st century church can no longer rely upon a legacy of cultural religiosity to ensure their continuing presence in the world. Christianity continually appears to be headed towards becoming the "alternative lifestyle" for much of the Western world. "The institutional church in the next twenty years will continue

---

[109] James Engel, *Changing the Mind of Missions*, (Downers Grove, IL: InterVarsity Press, 2000), p. 111.

[110] Kenneth Callahan, *Effective Church Leadership* (San Francisco: Jossey-Bass Publishers, 1990), p. 26

more and more to look like the pink Cadillac with the huge tail fins."[111] Even the Roman Catholic Church[112] and World Council of Churches have recognized the urgent need of evangelism and are now giving greater attention to what has always traditionally consumed the energies of evangelical Christians.[113] "Ours is not as we once imagined a secular society, it is a pagan society and its paganism having been born out of the rejection of Christianity is far more resistant to the gospel than the pre-Christian paganism with which cross-cultural missions have been familiar."[114] (The fact that the United States is now considered a mission field by many missiologists is not an original view with me. This impression has been greatly elaborated on in depth by prominent authors such as Lesslie Newbigin,[115] Craig Van Gelder,[116] David Bosch,[117] and Wilbert Shenk[118]).

The postmodern era for the United States is not a completely hopeless scenario. Potentially, we can even see the glass as half full if we can transition into a missional ethos and properly equip our congregations through appropriate and relevant evangelism training. However, a missional approach will certainly require a more demanding role for the local

---

[111] Leonard Sweet, *Postmodern Pilgrims*, p. 2.

[112] On September 5, 2000 "the Vatican released a thirty-six page declaration which called on Catholic religious workers and missionaries to resist the 'so called theology of religious pluralism,' saying it endangers the Church's missionary message." *Scottsdale Tribune*, "Catholic Decree Draws Concern" 8 September 2000, A1.

[113] Kenneth Boyack, *Catholic Evangelization Today: A New Pentecost for the United States* (New York: Paulist Publishers, 1987).

[114] Lesslie Newbigin, *Foolishness to the Greeks* (Grand Rapids: Eerdmans, 1986) p. 20.

[115] Lesslie Newbigin, *The Gospel in a Pluralistic Society* (Grand Rapids: Eerdmans, 1989).

[116] George Hunsberger and Craig Van Gelder, *The Church between Gospel and Culture* (Grand Rapids: Eerdmans, 1986).

[117] David Bosch, *Transforming Mission: Paradigm Shifts in Theology of Mission* (New York: Orbis Books, 1991).

[118] Wilbert Shenk, "The Culture of Modernity as a Missionary Challenge" in *The Church between Gospel and Culture*.

church. Missionaries know that success in cross-cultural communication requires patience and care in how we approach each culture. A hasty approach towards cross-cultural missions is not only a disastrous situation for the first pioneer missionary but also creates an obstacle for all future endeavors. Missions experts (missiologists) are very mindful of the need for careful research, building trust and relationships within the community, and fluency in the local language.[119] These same aspects will be needed if the local church in North America is going to truly permeate our culture with the Gospel.

It's easy for us as Christians to completely overlook the fact that we live in an entirely different subculture as compared to our secular neighbors and friends. North American Christianity has its own music, television channels, movies, language, and bookstores. We no longer share the same Judeo-Christian heritage, values or beliefs as our neighbors. They speak and think much differently from the unchurched modernist. As a result, new methodologies will be needed for reaching them as well as a willingness by the church to explore new methods for personal evangelism.

There are two essential elements that are critical in achieving this paradigm shift: First, we need to take seriously our new situation while we still have a strong Christian core within North America by developing missionary methodologies that will permeate the postmodern context; and secondly, we need to be able to effectively and properly train our congregations for personal evangelism within a postmodern context. "If Peter Drucker has taught us one thing, it is that every organization exists to serve people outside the organization."[120] Erwin McManus, pastor of Mosaic Church in Los Angeles says, "We somehow think that the Church is here for us; we forget that we are the Church, and we're here for the

---

[119] This is referred to as contextualization. Possibly two of the best examples for demonstrating the effectiveness of contextualization are Patrick (Ireland) and Hudson Taylor (China).

[120] Leonard Sweet, *Carpe Manana* (Grand Rapids: Zondervan, 2001), p. 28.

world." Due to the fact that we do have a "Christian" heritage and a strong core of churches we can possibly capitalize on the current "spiritual curiosity" *if* we act quickly. Otherwise, we will probably experience the same marginalization that occurred in Asia Minor and North Africa following the Crusades.

Developing a missional approach to evangelizing North America will require a complete overhaul in the ethos and purpose of nearly all Protestant churches. Generally, most churches tend to have distinguishing strengths and niches. Many are even well known in their communities for their music, Bible teaching, children's programming, pastor, etc. These same churches are often even staffed to maintain these distinguishing traits that reflect the ethos of the church. There is nothing amiss with churches developing strengths in particular areas. In fact, it tends to be the result of God's specific calling and gifting of individual leaders and congregations. However, in order to develop a missional approach, these strengths need to be used as a vehicle for introducing the surrounding community to the Gospel and they cannot simply be a means unto themselves.

A missional approach requires that every program and ministry be placed first through the Great Commission filter (i.e., Is this program or event a culturally acceptable vehicle for introducing the gospel or making disciples?). This is not to say that every single facet of church life be evangelistic, that would also be unhealthy, but it does mean that in addition to edification, each program and ministry have an evangelistic goal in mind. Yes, this sounds a little radical, but this is what's needed if we are going to adopt a missional ethos and become intentionally evangelistic. "Because God is a missionary God, God's people are to be missionary people. The church's mission is not secondary to its being; the church exists in being sent and in building itself up for its mission."[121] Therefore, it is essential that the local church possess a mission statement

---

[121] David Bosch, *Believing in the Future*, p. 32.

that reflects its missiological purpose. The mission statement should simply answer the question: Why are we doing this? Every member of the congregation should be able to clearly state the reason for its existence and know that it's responsible for implementing the Great Commission (evangelism and edification) to its' community.

A major part of the problem with churches in North America is that they have been around so long that they have lost sight of the primary purpose for which they were created in the first place.

> Simply asking a member the question, 'What are we trying to do? will often evoke blank and puzzled stares that seem to say, 'We're not trying to do anything-we're a church for goodness' sake!' On the other end of the spectrum, some people will respond with an entire laundry list...teach people...build up the body of Christ...worship and grow...help needy people in the community and send missionaries overseas.' These aren't bad goals, but they are ordered by a stream of consciousness, not by a clear sense of mission or priority.[122]

Rick Warren feels that one of the primary reasons for the success and growth of Saddleback Community Church in Lake Forest, California was the willingness of the congregation to process every church-related event through the grid of their purpose statement. "Nothing precedes purpose. The starting point for every church should be the question, 'Why do we exist?' Until you know what your church exists for, you have no foundation, no motivation, and no direction for ministry."[123] Along similar lines, Bill Hull says,

> "We must first teach leaders to have a theology of mission. Then they can develop a mental image of how to accomplish

---

[122] Mark Mittleberg, *Building a Contagious Church*, p. 24.
[123] Rick Warren, *The Purpose Driven Church* (Grand Rapids: Zondervan, 1995), p. 80-81.

the mission through working models. Our training must set forth the principles of leadership, people development, and evangelism, just as Paul espoused for the corporate church in Eph. 4:11–16. Working models provide the illustration of the principle. When a working model is not principle-based, a serious flaw emerges. If you want short-term results, rely on models. If you desire long-term results, and a continual stream of emerging, working models, begin with a foundation of philosophical principles."[124]

However, a simple "statement of faith" alone is not sufficient for incorporating a missional ethos. Although it is vital that the congregation know its purpose, it is ineffectual and irrelevant if it is not actually practiced by the congregation.

> While a statement of faith or official doctrinal position is vital to a congregation's reason to exist, it is incomplete without a functional theology of mission. The official doctrinal statement tells us why we are here; the theology of mission addresses the question, 'Now what?' Apart from a disciple's internal struggles with the world, the flesh, and the devil, a lack of theology of mission is the primary reason for church sloth and decline. It manifests itself in a lack of vision and strategy.[125]

Mittelberg complements this by noting the importance and necessity for the local church to be *intentionally* evangelistic.

> One thing's for sure: without intentional planning, decision making, and leadership-and a whole lot of course corrections along the way-a church ministry will never experience sustained evangelistic fruitfulness. This is not something churches drift

---

[124] David Hull, *Can We Save the Evangelical Church?*, p. 32.
[125] David Hull, *Ibid*, p. 29.

into on their own. No, building a contagious church only happens on purpose! A carefully developed plan, along with supporting values and action steps, must be in place before a church can become truly effective at reaching lost people for Christ.[126]

In most evangelical circles today, personal evangelism is optional, although hinted at in its mission statement. Somehow, it has become an elective when it should be as natural as prayer, worship, Bible study, and fellowship. In a "missional" context, the Church exists primarily to make disciples of its community, which necessitates personal evangelism. This must be the mission and the purpose of the local church if it strives to become a mission outpost within a postmodern society. This requires a back to basics mentality. Supposedly, Vince Lombardi, the legendary coach of the Green Bay Packers once said, "Gentlemen, this is a football," to a group of men who had already been making a living playing professional football. Likewise, the church needs to practice the very basics by defining, "Gentlemen, this is a church and our mission is to make disciples locally and globally."

The church has been called to the unique task of proclaiming the Good News (Mt. 28:19, 20). It is not called to be a political organization, social, nor even a community center. It *is* called to preach the gospel and to equip the saints for the work of ministry (Eph. 4:11, 12). Today, the pagans are in our own backyard and while we still need to go to the uttermost parts of the earth with the gospel; more than ever before, we must reach our Jerusalems. "An effective missionary congregation...not only seeks to fulfill its mission, it also seeks its survival and growth."[127]

In seeking to translate the gospel into postmodernese, we take our turn in church history in spreading the good news in a relevant manner to a

---

[126] Mark Mittelberg, *Building A Contagious Church* (Grand Rapids: Zondervan, 2000), pp. 17, 18.

[127] John Huegli, "Riding the Waves of Change" in *Confident Witness*, p. 285.

new generation. The process of translation holds the promise that not only that the postmodern generation will have an understanding of the gospel but that they will also be transformed by it and then translate the Good News to their world.

Chapter 11

Postmodern Apologetics

Recently it has been suggested that a presentation of the gospel which is centered on propositional revelation is an error for postmodern evangelism purposes. This position has been advocated by Michael Polanyi, Stanley Grenz and Alister McGrath.[128] McGrath says, "Any view of revelation which regards God's self-disclosure as the mere transmission of facts concerning God is seriously deficient, and risks making God an analogue of a corporate executive who disperses memoranda to underlings."[129]

In *A Primer on Postmodernism*, Grenz says,

> "[We] cannot simply collapse truth into the categories of rational certainty that typify modernity. Rather, in understanding and articulating the Christian faith, we must

> "Postmodernism must be confronted, not accommodated. We must challenge its false presuppositions, lovingly explaining that there is truth and that it is knowable."
>
> —Charles Colson

---

[128] See Michael Polanyi, *Personal Knowledge: Towards a Post Critical Philosophy* (London: Routers & Kegal Press, 1988).
[129] Alister McGrath, *A Passion for Truth*, p. 106.

make room for the concept of "mystery"—not as an irrational complement to the rational but as a reminder that the fundamental reality of God transcends human rationality. While remaining reasonable, therefore, the appeal of our gospel must not be limited to the intellectual aspect of the human person. It must encompass other dimensions of our being as well."[130]

Grenz has accurately assessed that we need to make room for mystery in order to avoid a spirit of triumphalism. This can be accomplished in evangelism training by making room for "I don't know" and yet we must simultaneously be as apologetically prepared as possible for addressing their concerns and misunderstandings because, as Groothuis says, "If Christians defensively cloak themselves in mystery without evoking logic, they lose their ability to criticize other worldviews."[131] The 21st century Christian must be able to utilize both objective and subjective tools for proclaiming and defending the Christian worldview.

This creates a tension in which we must not come across with a "know it all" persona and yet simultaneously we must equip our congregations to anticipate particular intellectual roadblocks and even politely challenge the worldview foundations of the non-believer. In spite of postmodernism, the utilization of truth claims for presenting the gospel is still an essential component that cannot be ignored nor compromised. (This is not to suggest that Grenz and McGrath advocate such a drastic abandonment of reason in personal evangelism). Although Grenz and McGrath are to be applauded for thinking outside of the box in seeking a non-rationalistic approach for evangelizing postmoderns for the sake of reaching them where they are, a complete abandonment of rational methodologies for evangelizing the postmodern would be an overreaction.

"Most people, including academics, think that there is no objective truth. No one uses a postmodernist hermeneutic when reading the label of

---

[130] Grenz, *A Postmodern Primer*, p. 170.
[131] Groothuis, *Truth Decay*, p. 124.

a medicine bottle. Theologians tend to think that postmodern pluralism and relativism are all the rage, when in fact such thinking is largely confined to the literature, social sciences, and religious studies department at universities."[132]

However, it is obvious that postmodernists are able to live with these types of contradictions and it is of utmost importance that Christians avoid a condescending presentation when utilizing truth claims.[133] In spite of an acknowledgement that we cannot know exhaustive truth, God has equipped us with the ability to know some truth or "true truth" as Francis Schaeffer liked to say. Grenz's assessment that we live in a post-rationalistic culture is obvious, but what he fails to produce is substantial evidence on the effectiveness of a non-rationalistic approach regarding personal evangelism. Perhaps (hopefully) it is forthcoming.

Christian evangelism, or any type of proselytizing, is naturally seen as a ludicrous and ignorant endeavor in the postmodern view, because truth itself is relative which, of course, is contrary to the Christian claim that there is absolute truth. However, Mark Mittelberg points out that we should not be led to believe that the postmodernist doesn't care about truth:

> Many people today have become increasingly relativistic, thinking there are many 'truths' but being highly skeptical of anything claiming to be 'Truth.' Among the younger generations, people tend to be more experiential in their approach to deciding what to believe. They don't generally lead off with questions about scientific or empirical verification. They're often more pragmatic

---

[132] William Lane Craig in *Five Views On Apologetics*, ed. Steven Cowan (Grand Rapids: Zondervan, 2000), p. 181.

[133] Inconsistency and contradiction are viable lifestyles within the postmodern worldview because consistency may be classified as an oppressive Western metanarrative.

and search out what seems to be working in the lives of their friends and others they respect. But give these people some time, and earn their trust. Once the layers are peeled back, many of the classic questions will begin to surface-along with a few new ones. The issues are often the same, but the people raising them usually have far less knowledge about God and the Bible than those of past generations.[134]

Being equipped to anticipate and address the most common concerns has the two-fold benefit of developing confidence in the believer while simultaneously enhancing their understanding of the postmodern culture. According to internal surveys, one of the primary reasons Christians do not get involved in sharing their faith is that they are afraid that they will be asked a question that they cannot answer. Therefore, to aid in removing this barrier, it is beneficial to equip the participants beforehand on some of the most frequently asked questions.

"While apologetics needs to be *truth-centered*, it must also be *person sensitive* and *culturally aware*. Unbelievers come to the table with a variety of issues, misconceptions and values that need to be discerned before a fruitful apologetic can occur. The truths for which we argue are not relative, but the level of knowledge of our hearers is relative and must be taken into account."[135] As Mittelberg says:

> "As soon as the topic of faith comes up, many people have a list of doubts and concerns (that) pop into their minds. 'How can I be sure God even exists?' There are so many religions, how can I have confidence any of them is really true?' 'Can't I just worship God by myself, out in the woods?' 'If God really cares about us, why would he let me go through so many awful things in my life?' Furthermore, we must also be prepared to defend the very

---

[134] Mark Mittelberg, *Building A Contagious Church*, p. 262.
[135] Groothuis, *Truth Decay*, p. 184.

existence of truth itself. These and similar questions form what I call *intellectual road blocks* that prevent persons from taking steps forward in their spiritual journey. If we want to help people move toward Christ, we are going to have to proactively address their issues and show that the Christian faith is built on a foundation of truth and can be trusted wholeheartedly."[136]

Some of the typical spiritual roadblocks that a postmodernist may have are:
- "Isn't it arrogant for Christians to claim that Jesus is the only way?"
- "Don't all religions basically teach the same thing and just use different names for God?"
- "Why would a holy God allow evil and suffering?"
- "As long as a person is genuinely sincere, what difference does it make?"
- "What about people who have never even heard of Jesus? Do they go to Hell?"

- "I don't believe in the existence of truth."
- "Isn't the Bible full of errors and contradictions, not to mention outdated?"
- "Why is Christianity homophobic and oppressive to women?"
- "What about evolution?"
- "How come Christians don't care about the environment?"
- "What about UFOs?"
- "What about the 'Matrix theory?"

So, how do we respond to these? While space is not permitted here to comprehensively address all of these questions, I would like to provide a

---

[136] Mittelberg, *Building A Contagious Church*, p. 42.

few concise responses. I highly encourage you to invest some time into the works of scholars like Lee Strobel, Ravi Zacharias, Gary Habermas, Norman Geisler, J.P. Mooreland, Josh McDowell, and Francis Schaeffer in order to do justice to these questions. (I hope that we can anticipate more volumes from contemporary scholars to address the following issues). After you have researched these issues, you should transfer what you've learned into the discipleship process of those within your tutelage in order that your sheep do not get swallowed whole by the postmodern wolves. You may also want to consider offering a special class on Sundays at your church to address the primary obstacles that postmoderns have regarding Christianity. At our church I designed a special course that was somewhat of a Christian version of the *Dead Poets Society* for the express purpose of dealing with some of these topics. In order to equip your church for evangelizing a postmodern culture, you should consider offering a class or elective that deals with some of the following issues:

Isn't it arrogant for Christians to claim that Jesus is the only way?

Due to postmodernism's hypersensitivity to political correctness, exclusivism is often portrayed as a form of spiritual racism. Philosophically, however, the assertion that other and/or many ways lead to God is a violation of the Law of Non-Contradiction. Simply put, we cannot all be right because we're all proclaiming different teachings for salvation. It was Jesus Christ who made the statement "I am the Way, the Truth, and The Life. No one comes to the Father except through me" (John 14:6), thus, their argument is essentially with Jesus himself.

As followers of Christ, we are simply espousing His teachings regarding this issue. Nevertheless, unlike any other religious leader, Jesus Christ alone has the credentials to back up this claim. He regularly made it clear that He was God and possessed the evidence to substantiate his claim with miracles, prophecies, a sinless life, and an empty tomb. Therefore, the exclusive nature of salvation is a revelation of truth and therefore it is not arrogant. Rather, thinking that we can somehow earn or merit salvation through our works and deeds is arrogance. For further study consider reading *The Case for Christ* by Lee Strobel and *More than a Carpenter* by Josh McDowell.

Don't all religions basically teach the same things and just use different names for God?

No. This is a very common misperception. It only takes about ten minutes of research to discover that, Christianity has very little in common with any of the other religions. The general perception is that all religious people are moral people who pray and read some form of a sacred writing. Although we generally do share these attributes, our doctrines of salvation, creation, eschatology, the after-life, and Jesus Christ are contradictory and thus violates the law of non-contradiction.

There are two primary and vital differences to consider.[137] The first is in regard to Jesus Christ. Islam teaches that Jesus was a prophet of God, but not the Son of God. Buddhism and Hinduism both believe in reincarnation. Some branches of Buddhism don't even believe in a personal God, whereas Hinduism teaches that everything, including the paper for this book is God. Judaism teaches that Jesus was a teacher, rabbi, and maybe a prophet, but not the Messiah. Jehovah Witnesses don't believe in the Trinity and Mormonism teaches that you too can become a god, just like Jesus did and have your own planet. Therefore, as you can see, there is a vast chasm regarding Jesus.

---

[137] The Virgin Birth of Jesus Christ (Incarnation); The Bodily Resurrection of Jesus Christ; The Second Coming of Jesus Christ; Inspiration of Scripture, and God the Author of Creation are a few others.

Secondly, there is the doctrine of salvation. As Bill Hybels says, it's about "Do vs. Done"[138] Religion is the hypothesis that we can somehow work our way into favor with God through works, acts of compassion, etc. and thus it is about doing works. Therefore, it implies that there is some sort of a "cosmic morality gauge" that determines one's eligibility for everlasting life. Interestingly, the postmodernist in implying that there is a "good" is an acknowledgement that an absolute must exist by which one is measured.

Christianity, however, is spelled "Done" because Jesus Christ, being God, was the only eligible candidate to pay the price for our sins. He lived the perfect life we could never live and on the Cross he paid for our sins. Therefore, Christianity is spelled "DONE." This is the key difference between Christianity and all other religions. Religion is about doing some set of works and deeds in order to merit forgiveness, everlasting life, etc. Jesus, on the other hand, offers a personal relationship to God that is grace-based.

Why would a holy God allow evil and suffering?

Please be mindful that these are deep questions and I cannot begin to give them justice in a few paragraphs, but let me encourage you to always lend a sympathetic ear to all of these questions and to avoid a "know-it-all" type attitude. It has been my experience that this particular question is often asked due to a personal experience such as a miscarriage, a loved one killed by a drunk driver, etc.

Suffering is a topic that God can relate to. His own innocent Son died a horrific and gruesome death at the hand of sinners. Essentially, in order for mankind to have the ability to choose necessitates that he/she have the capability to be able to make the wrong choice. Otherwise we would be a

---

[138] Bill Hybels, *Becoming A Contagious Christian* (Grand Rapids: Zondervan, 1994), p. 155-156.

mindless race of robots. (Interestingly, even the angels were given the option to obey or rebel against God.) Actually, the vast majority of evil in this world is actually perpetuated by humans sinning against humans. God has done something about evil in that he offers redemption through Jesus Christ and He has also promised to return to earth to make things right. Justice delayed is not justice deferred.

As long as a person is genuinely sincere, what difference does it make?

The difference is that the object of a person's faith may be misdirected and misinformed. There was a time when people sincerely believed that the earth was flat and that the sun rotated around the earth. They were sincere in their beliefs but they were sincerely wrong. Therefore, sincerity does not automatically result in validity.

What about all the people who have never heard about Jesus? Do they go to hell?

If you are a Calvinist, the answer is rather simple: God knows who will place their faith in Him and He will ensure that they have a hearing of the Gospel. However, the typical postmodernist could care less about our theology. First of all, we don't know for absolute certain that they haven't heard. Nearly 2 billion people have now seen the *Jesus* film. Secondly, if the person asking this question knows of an unreached group on the planet kindly ask them to identify the group. If they can identify an unevangelized people group, challenge them to consider taking the gospel there because the individual raising the question *has* heard. I realize that this sounds like somewhat of a tongue and cheek answer but the point is to direct the conversation back to the fact that the person you are interacting with has had a hearing. Jesus Christ has commissioned us to take the gospel to the uttermost parts of the earth (Mt. 28: 19, 20; Acts 1:8) and this is something that we will probably have to give an account for at the Judgment Seat of Christ.

The question of unreached people groups is a challenging and difficult question. For one, it is very humbling in that we have been blessed with a hearing of the gospel. I'm aware that issues such as predestination often surface here and the Calvinistic response is typically something like "God knows who will place their faith in him and he will ensure that they have a hearing of the Gospel." Likewise, I once heard Billy Graham say in an interview that "the more people I witness to the more people become predestined." However, such explanations are confusing to a culture that is "ignorant of Christian doctrine and beliefs" and we should stick to apologetics rather than theology at this stage. The postmodernist could care less about our in-house squabbles and dilemmas. However, it's important that we assure them that the fate of these people groups rests in the hands of a holy and loving God and that he is well aware of their unevangelized condition and then refocus the conversation on the fact that they have heard.

Sometimes it is worth pointing out that the global population of 35 A.D. is estimated to be approximately 200 Million. Therefore, mathematically, if the 5,000 new believers from Pentecost were faithful in just telling one person a week (without any conversions) about the gospel, it would've taken about a decade to spread the Good News. I realize the improbability of this, but nevertheless, it does demonstrate that it wasn't an impossible task.

The New Testament presents an extremely Christocentric view of salvation and even emphasizes that salvation is through the Son. Acts 4:12 stresses that there is "no other name" by which men can be saved. Of course, this is not a popular answer for postmodern ears, but when pressed, we must trust God with the truth and avoid the temptation to soften the gospel for the sake of telling them what they want to hear. Rather, we can kindly refocus the conversation on the fact that they have heard the gospel, discuss the credentials of Jesus Christ, his unique eligibility to offer salvation, and share how he has transformed our lives.

I don't believe in the existence of truth?

This is a self-refuting statement because by their own admission they are stating a truth claim in that they believe in at least one truth (that there is no truth). We can agree with the postmodernist that there is mystery and that we cannot know exhaustive truth. However, this does not necessitate the fact that we cannot know any truth at all. We can know with certainty, for example, a vast array of material in the fields of mathematics, physics, geometry, engineering, geography, biology, etc. Furthermore, we can demonstrate, for example, that A is A and A is not non-A. That is, Paris is either the capitol of France or it is not.

Furthermore, "To say that God communicates truly does not mean that God communicates exhaustively. Even in our human relationships we never have exhaustive communication, though what we do have may be true."[139] Biblical Christianity is a distinct way, established and ordained by God for knowing the Truth. Although it is not completely sufficient, reason can be reliable.

Personally, I believe in applying a rather direct and slightly confrontational approach in this case by challenging them to see the absurdity of this argument by simply asking them a series of practical questions such as: Do you stop at red lights in a busy intersection? Is there a basketball team that is known as the Phoenix Suns? The point is not to insult their intelligence. Rather, it is to make obvious the laughable and unlivability of such a profession and to shake the foundations of their worldview.

---

[139] Francis Schaeffer, *The God Who is There*, p. 119.

Isn't the Bible full of errors, not to mention outdated?

The classic response is to ask the questioner, "Can you show me one?" with the hope that the questioner will be dumbfounded and unable to produce such an instance. In most cases it is true that the person asking this question is simply repeating something that they have heard on a talk show or in a movie and not demonstrated. I still think that asking the postmodernist to point out the occurrence that they have in mind is an appropriate response as long as it is not done in a smug way. For example, I like to humbly reply, "I've read the Bible a number of times and I don't recall seeing any. Can you provide me with an example? Perhaps I can help."

However, anticipate that the well-educated postmodernist may have an apparent discrepancy to point out to you. Therefore, if you are uncertain of an apparent contradiction, be humble enough to admit that you are uncertain but assure them that you will do some research and follow up on their question. The fact that you may not be able to answer the question at hand that particular moment does not mean that there is not an answer. With a little research you'll be able to help them overcome what may be a spiritual hurdle. Likewise, equip yourself to defend the authenticity of Scriptures and their uniqueness among all other Sacred writings. Briefly, let me add, that Scripture does declare itself to be inspired (2 Tim 3:16 and 1 Peter 2:20, 21) whereas the vast majority of all non-Christian "sacred writings" make no such claim. Likewise, there is substantial manuscript evidence, archaeological confirmations, documented prophecies, and eye-witness accounts that overwhelmingly confirm Scripture's credibility.

Another postmodern argument regarding the Bible's credibility is the suggestion that it's original meaning has been lost due to the numerous translations and versions. Again, the scenario here is typically that of a postmodern simply reciting a mantra that they heard in college. However, rarely have they ever taken the time to investigate or research the matter.

Although it is true that there are numerous translations and versions, this is actually an argument confirming the authenticity of the Bible, because they are all communicating the same message. Additionally, the discovery of the Dead Sea scrolls confirmed that we have in our hands the same translations that were being used by the Essenes over 2,000 years ago.

A person is simply misinformed to conclude that we cannot know the true meaning of the Bible because there are so many interpretations. While there may be many interpretations, there can only be one correct one—the message of the original author to his intended audience. This is why, for example, we have the discipline of hermeneutics. For further reading consult *The Journey from Texts to Translations: The Origin and Development of the Bible* by Paul Wegner and *Is There Meaning in this Text?* by Kevin Vanhoozer.

Why is Christianity homophobic and oppressive towards women?

We cannot deny that there are some groups, who under the Christian umbrella, portray the perception that Christians hate homosexuals. Typically, however, homosexual activists try to tag anyone who disapproves of the homosexual lifestyle or their agenda as "homophobic." This, of course, is unfair, hypocritical, and simply inaccurate. It is true that Scripture does not condone homosexual relationships. However, we must remember that God's instructions and prohibitions are largely for the welfare of His creation. Therefore, as a part of God's creation we trust that He knows what's best for humanity and accept His wisdom regarding this issue. Although it sounds cliché it is true that this is a case where we, as believers, hate the sin, but not the sinner.

In regards to women, in the first book of the Bible, we are told that God created both male and female in his image (Gen 1: 27). The fact that some functions and roles for family life and ecclesiastical positions are different is a testament to our uniqueness and giftedness. Jesus. Jesus Christ was revolutionary in that he regularly used women as examples in his teachings and interacted with them in a time and society in which women were often treated like property. Women, for example, were the first humans to see him following his resurrection. It is true that many "Christians" today still do not seem to value women in the way that Jesus did, but such an attitude would be contrary to the ministry of Jesus Christ. Thus, based on the above it can easily be argued that Jesus viewed women as equal to men, especially in the ways in which he affirmed and elevated them in a culture that generally did not.

What about evolution?

Typically, the postmodernist has been educated that evolution is factual and not a theory and that consequently it disproves God, the Bible, and Creationism. Evolution still has not been demonstrated in a laboratory experiment and there is still no evidence of a species changing from one to another in the fossil record. In fact, the evidence is overwhelming in favor of creationism rather than randomness. As Hank Hanegraaff says, "Darwin had an excuse. In his day fossil finds were relatively scarce. Today, however, more than a century after his death…we have an abundance of fossils. Still, we have yet to find even one legitimate transition from one species to another."[140] The burden of proof remains with the evolutionist.

Dr. Walter Brown[141] believes that many evolutionists are starting to see the cracks in the foundation of evolution, but are reluctant to admit it due to job security and research grants. Likewise, there may be somewhat of a pride factor due to the fact that their doctorates are often hinged on the theory. Regardless, it is important that we study to show ourselves

---

[140] Hank Hanegraaff, *The Face that Demonstrates the Farce of Evolution* (Nashville: Word Publishing, 1998), p. 33.

[141] Visit www.creationscience.com for more information on Creation Science.

approved in this area in order that we can intelligently discuss the issues. Several authors such as Hanegraaff, Walt Brown, Phillip Johnson, and Hugh Ross have written in-depth and scholarly articles and books dealing with the false theory of evolution. Our goal is to use apologetics as a vehicle for ultimately presenting the gospel. We must always remember to take the conversation back to Jesus Christ. It is irrelevant as to whether or not a person believes in a young or old earth for salvation. It is absolutely essential that they believe in Jesus for their salvation (Rom 10:9).

How come Christians don't care about the environment?

It is somewhat interesting and yet unfortunate that non-believers have initiated some of the more pressing social concerns of the postmodern era. Environmentalism, to a degree, is. In Gen 1:28 God ordained humanity to be caretakers of the earth meaning that we have been tasked with caring for and utilizing the earth and its resources wisely and in service to God and humanity. I believe that the reason that it is not a focus of evangelical Christianity is for the simple fact that within the Christian worldview we are correctly focused on the Great Commission (Mt. 28:19,20). Nevertheless, this is not an excuse to ignore environmental concerns, while simultaneously it cannot become the focus of our outreach ministries. So, what should we do? We can start by making our own churches "green friendly" by providing receptacles for recycling paper and aluminum. We can make a difference by using a mug, rather than paper cup, for our daily coffee. Even most coffee shops will gladly refill your own personal mug for you. Consider recruiting some people from your Sunday School class to participate in the "Adopt-a-Street" program.

Get creative. There are a number of things that we can do to show that, as Christians, we do care about our planet and that we are at least doing something, rather than nothing, about it. Within our Christian worldview, its easy to "let the pagans save the cans", but if we are going to build bridges and friendships with postmoderns we must pay more than lip service to the environment. In fact, I see this as a great way for the church to have something in common with them since they perceive pollution, etc as a moral issue. Put together a team at your church that will prayerfully implement some ways to help your church become more environmentally friendly.[142]

What about UFOs?

Personally, I believe that the UFO phenomenon is the Darwinism of the 21st century. In the same way that Christians scoffed at *Origin of Species* in 1859, 21st century Christians scoff at this postmodern concern. The fact of the matter is that the belief in Extra-terrestrial life has gained broader acceptance in the scientific community in the past 20 years and is considered a legitimate subject in most space exploration circles. Nevertheless, the point is that to date there is no evidence for extraterrestrial life. None. In fact, the more we learn about the universe the more we learn how very unique our solar system is.

Nevertheless, we must learn from the "Copernicus Incident" and not be too dogmatic on scientific issues in which the Bible is silent. If they do exist, God is their creator too (Gen. 1:1). Regardless, the burden of proof remains with ETI proponents. The written revelation that we do have from God (Bible) as well as the ministry of Jesus Christ are both focused upon humanity's need for redemption.[143]

---

[142] Consider reading *Pollution and the Death of Man* by Francis Schaeffer.
[143] This issue will be discussed in-depth in the forthcoming *UFOs: 10 Things You Should Know* by Bobby Brewer in 2003.

"What about the Matrix Theory?"

As ludicrous as it may seem, this is an objection that is taken seriously by some postmodernists. Simply put, the theory is that, as popularized in the movie Matrix, we can never know for certain what is real. As the encounter in the Preface describes, these types sincerely believe that we should not rely upon our five senses to determine reality.[144] For a postmodern that is a purist my goal is to often move them just one step closer to being a seeker of Christ. That is, if the person is an atheist, my goal may be to move them from being an atheist into being a cynic or skeptic. Personally, I really like to have fun with these types of postmodernists by suggesting that, since we cannot know for certain what's real, if they would be willing to give me $1000 in exchange for $1. If its not real, what should it matter? Or in the event of an emergency blood transfusion, would it be necessary to know what blood type they would need or would any type do? Then I take a more serious direction by asking if we should do away with laws and release all of the serial killers? The goal is to show them that there are some things we can know for certain and the unlivability and immorality of their a worldview. Of course, do not forget to politely shift the burden of proof to them by asking them to provide evidence that we cannot know some things with certainty.

The Joshua Challenge

One of the advantages of postmodernism is that it allows us to freely engage in spiritual conversations in which we can politely challenge the religious beliefs of those that we have built relationships with. Too often, Christians are on the defensive and entrenched in spiritual fox holes when, like Joshua, we should be carrying the battle forward and claiming new

---

[144] See page xiii.

ground in articulating the gospel while simultaneously helping the postmodernist comprehend their false presumptions. Socrates (470–399 B.C.) described this as "patient questioning." "By asking specific questions that challenged his students' assumptions, Socrates led them into a kind of self-discovery. They concluded for themselves the error of their existing beliefs and went on to accept a new or a different conclusion."[145]

Francis Schaeffer utilized a very similar strategy that he referred to as "taking the roof off" in that he would press a person to see the unlivability of their professed world view by pushing them towards it's logical conclusion. "We ought not to try first to move a man away from the logical conclusion of his position but towards it."[146] Schaeffer's goal was to expose the unlivability of any non-Christian world view. (Interestingly, he counseled believers to proceed cautiously when implementing this strategy with an existentialist because their logical conclusion may result in suicidal tendencies). Dan Story provides an excellent example of this apologetic method in his book, *Engaging the Closed Mind*, and provides the following questions for confronting unbelievers to confront the illegitimacy of their spiritual beliefs:

- "How do you know that?"
- "What evidence do you have for that?"
- "Where did you learn that?"
- "On what authority do you base your view?"
- "What happens if you're wrong?"
- "Have you ever considered…?"
- "In light of what you believe, how would you explain…?"

---

[145] Dan Story, *Engaging the Closed Mind* (Grand Rapids: Kregel Publications, 1999), p. 67.
[146] Schaeffer, *The God Who Is There*, p. 156.

- "Where did you learn that all religions are true?"
- What happens if you're wrong, and all religions don't lead to God?"[147]

Story also introduces the utilization of what he calls "Boomerang Questions" in which he suggests that we challenge non-believers with the same questions that they often ask us: "How do *you* explain the presence of pain and suffering?" "How do you know your holy book is true revelation?", etc.[148]

The goal here is to engage in spiritual conversations in which we will have the opportunity to first shake the foundations of their non-Christian world view and to then articulate the gospel in terms that they will comprehend. It behooves us here to follow the admonishment of Peter who said, "…Always be prepared to give an answer to everyone who asks you to give the reason for the hope that you have, but do this with gentleness and respect" (1 Peter 3:15).

---

[147] *Ibid*, p. 72-73.
[148] *Ibid*, p. 73

Chapter 12

Know Your Culutre, Know Your Niche

When Charles Haddon Spurgeon first went to Park Street Church in London, he was nineteen. There he found a church with a seating capacity of fifteen hundred but with an attendance under two hundred. Nine years later the Metropolitan Tabernacle was built to accommodate the crowds that were coming to hear him preach. His sermons were published in newspapers; he started a school (seminary) to train preachers; an orphanage was established; and a printing shop was established to print evangelistic booklets and tracts. It is estimated that approximately 23,000 people came through the doors of Metropolitan Tabernacle on any given Sunday during his tenure.

During his thirty-eight years as pastor of Metropolitan Tabernacle the congregation grew by an estimated 14,000 members and became one of the most influential congregations during the nineteenth century. However, less than seventy-five years later, the church averages about eighty-seven. "What happened to this once great influential church? In simple terms, it hadn't changed with the times. London had changed;

people had changed; but the church's approach to ministry had remained the same."[149] [150]

Popular outreach methods in the mid-20th century included handing out gospel tracts, door-to-door visitation, Youth for Christ Saturday Night Rallies, the "Romans Road", and "The Four Spiritual Laws." These methods were all effective in reaching their "modern" culture, but they simply were not geared for the postmodern. Even though we now minister in the postmodern age, most churches continue to reflect outreach models that clearly reflect targeting for reaching the Modernist. These models of evangelism were developed in a completely different age for reaching a different type of culture and thus they even have the potential to further alienate the postmodern. This leads to stress for Outreach leaders because programs that once worked in the past no longer yield the same results. Rather than beginning at point A and then proceeding to point B, with the postmodernist we may have to begin at point E and then come back to A before going to B. Essentially, we have to begin where they are at and not where we think that they should be. "[E]ach generation must be reached for Christ differently. If we are to pass the baton of a living faith in Jesus Christ on to the next generation, we must find ways of handing it off to them in ways whereby they can receive it."[151]

> "A great many people living today formed their identities in the context of old institutions that are now radically changing or disappearing altogether."
>
> —Chuck Smith, Jr. *The End of the World As We Know It*

---

[149] Gary McIntosh, *The Issachar Factor* (Nashville: Broadman & Holman), p. 8.

[150] Historically, methods of evangelism have changed over the years. In the 1800s the trend in America favored the camp meeting format which typically lasted for about ten days or more and were held in forested areas. In the 1900s the tent meeting replaced this methodology and in the 1950s Billy Graham became a catalyst for the stadium meetings.

[151] Leonard Sweet, *SoulTsunami* (Grand Rapids: Zondervan, 1999), p. 175.

A few decades ago, for example, personal evangelism could be very direct and hard-hitting. Its function was to remind people of what they had already heard and knew. Since substantial Judeo-Christian assumptions were prevalent even within the secular culture, the primary challenge was to get them to make a decision on this information. It could all happen in a single high-impact event such as going door-to-door and asking people if they were ready to make a decision to accept Christ.

> Christians often seek to evangelize others by starting with salvation, John 3:16 and the gospel message. Most people had some kind of church experience in their background, even if they did not have strong personal beliefs. But in today's post-Christian world, many people no longer even understand the meaning of crucial biblical terms. For example, the basic term *sin* makes no sense to people if they have no concept of a holy God who created us and who therefore has a right to require certain things of us. And if people don't understand sin, they certainly don't comprehend the need for salvation. Consequently, in today's world, beginning evangelism with the message of salvation is like starting a book in the middle-you don't know the characters, and you can't make sense of the plot.[152]

Robert Webber, says, "a style of Christianity successful for one era changes as another era begins. Those who remain committed to the old style of faith subsequently freeze that style in the particular culture in which it originated."[153] This becomes an easy trap to fall into because unless we're students of culture we can quickly find ourselves trusting in the successful methodologies of the past even when they've lost their effectiveness.

---

[152] Charles Colson, *How Now Shall We Live?* (Wheaton: Tyndale, 1999), p. 98.
[153] Robert Webber, *Ancient Future Faith*, p. 13.

When most of the current evangelistic resources were written their authors correctly assessed their culture. Just thirty years ago most people believed in a personal God and were somewhat confident that the Bible was God's Word. What was missing was only that people lacked a clear gospel presentation. Thus, "gospel tract" authors developed ways to present the basics of the gospel in a straightforward way. These were all excellent presentations of the Gospel and saw great results. There's no question that they are biblically based and that God used them to effectively communicate the Gospel. (To a degree they even remain a valuable resource for ministering to those in today's world who embody a more modern than postmodern mindset.) However, as great as their legacy is, these personal evangelism tools were not created with the postmodern in mind. As George Hunter said, "We do not honor our founders by blindly perpetuating in a changing world what they once did...we honor them by doing for our time and culture what they once did for theirs."[154]

The 21st century church is in need of new "containers" for presenting the Gospel. In *Aqua Church*, Leonard Sweet presents the following analogy:

> "Water is a liquid that fills the shape of any receptacle. As long as we trust the water and don't tamper with the recipe-don't dilute it, thicken it, or separate its ingredients-the content can remain the same while containers change...Every generation needs a shape that fist its own hands, its own soul...A lot of churches are languishing because they won't trust the gospel to fit and fill containers with handles they don't like."[155]

Of course, being aware of our culture is one thing, but getting a church to change *its'* culture and explore new containers can be challenging.

---

[154] George Hunter, *Church for the Unchurched* (Nashville: Abingdon, 1996), p. 67.
[155] Leonard Sweet, *Aqua Church* (Loveland, CO: Group Publishing, 1999), p. 29.

Change is never easy. Ed Dobson, for example, deliberately took an entire year just to prepare the very traditional Calvary Church for the very *thought* of a Saturday night seeker service.[156] Although very few church leaders would debate the fact that postmodernism has impacted our culture, suggesting that a church change its traditional components can easily become the catalyst for a church split, especially if they are unable to distinguish between theology and methodology.

To their credit, Campus Crusade has made modifications to its popular *Four Spiritual Laws* gospel tract that has the postmodernist in mind by adding the phrase "it's not that simple" to aid in demonstrating the intellectuality of the gospel. Therefore, it is critical that you know your niche. There are certain plants that can grow in Arizona that cannot grow in Virginia and vice-versa. Trying to grow bananas in Alaska would be an ill fated venture. Likewise, it's important that you know your church's soil. What grows well at your church and in your community? What works in Columbus, Ohio may or may not work in San Diego. Starbucks and Samuel Adams know their niche. Do you know yours? One very well known church in California, for example, plans on remaining focused on the baby boomers. The mentality of their leadership is that their church is already well equipped for ministering to this niche and since the boomers by far outweigh the Gen-Xers in population, they see no need to do a complete about face. Although I disagree with their lack of focus on Gen-X and postmodernism, this church, nevertheless, knows its niche. However, by not addressing postmodernism will this well known church be the next Metropolitan Tabernacle?

Chuck Smith Jr. says, "Not all churches are the same, nor should they be based on the same model. Not all churches have the access to the same resources, are located in the same socioeconomic environment, or have staffs with the same level of competency. To rubber stamp one church

---

[156] Ed Dobson, *Starting a Seeker Sensitive Service* (Grand Rapids: Zondervan, 1993), p. 24.

model over the entire globe is a mistake of modernity."[157] It is critical that each church know its culture and its strengths. Below are a few examples of some churches that know their niche.

Learning to Speak Postmodernese

Located in Tempe, Arizona, Bethany Community Church is making adjustments to better reach its community. As the result of a demographic survey on the community and church, BCC recognized that it wasn't very successful in reaching its immediate community due to the fact that the community was significantly younger than their average member. Therefore, one of their first steps was the addition of a second morning service that is contemporary in its worship style. This service was intentionally geared towards Generation-X and thus included a praise/worship band, drama, testimonies, and generally a topical message.

BCC felt that by providing these elements in a contemporary service they could satisfy the spiritual hunger of the postmodern culture by providing them an opportunity to "experience God." John Vawter, Senior Pastor at BCC, does not speak at the contemporary service because he feels that the speaker should be someone who can speak the "Gen-X" language. The goal of many foreign missions is to provide a pastor who is indigenous to the culture to shepherd the church. Likewise, Vawter feels that the pastor/teacher for the contemporary service should be indigenous as well. Needless to say, some members felt that the gospel had been compromised in the contemporary service and left the church as a result of the changes, but the church is experiencing growth and the contemporary service now has the larger attendance of the two services.

---

[157] Chuck Smith, Jr. *The End of the World...As We Know It* (Colorado Springs: Waterbook Press, 2001), p. 117.

Within the last several years BCC has also become intentionally evangelistic towards the postmodern. In 1999, a mailing was sent to 10,000 homes inviting the community to attend a "How to Teach Your Kids to Build Boundaries" seminar of which approximately 70% of the 100 who attended were non-believers. BCC also conducts an annual outreach steak dinner in the spring in which members are encouraged to invite a non-believing friend to attend. At the dinner a Gospel presentation is delivered by a speaker that is recognizable within the community such as an athlete, celebrity, etc. Vawter feels that the steak dinner is one of their very best evangelistic tools because it helps in eliminating many of the false perceptions about Christianity while simultaneously demonstrating the life changing experience in the life of the speaker. It brings down preconceived barriers when they see that the "Christian" speaker is a real person with real problems like everyone else. According to Zander, "to win busters, we must overcome the negative caricature of Christianity that many of them hold."[158] As a result of discovering its niche and culture, BCC is experiencing new convert growth.

A New Method for an Established Church

About 20 miles north of BCC is somewhat of a different world. Whereas Tempe is primarily known for Arizona State University and its dense population of college students, Scottsdale is generally associated with wealth and prestige. At a staff retreat the pastors all agreed that they wanted and needed to become intentionally evangelistic. Scottsdale Bible Church has lived up to its name as a Bible church and is well known for its strong Bible teaching, yet evangelism, they concurred had not been a strong emphasis because there had never really been a problem with

---

[158] Marshall Shelly, *Growing Your Church through Evangelism and Outreach,* quoting Deter Zander in "The Gospel for Generation X," p. 56.

church growth at SBC. In fact, it regularly faces the dilemma of arrested development. Nevertheless, SBC provides an excellent example of how a well-established and largely traditional church can respond in reaching the postmodern culture through the worship service.

In order to become intentionally evangelistic SBC began offering invitations at the end of each of its five services. Acknowledging the postmodern culture, they opted for a new twist to the traditional "altar call" type of invitation. Rather than coming forward in front of 2000 plus people to accept Christ as Savior, non-believers were encouraged to pray the "sinners prayer" silently and to then raise their hands acknowledging their decision to the pastor. They were then instructed to visit the "Tell Me More" table on their way out of the worship center.[159] There, new believers receive a "spiritual gift pack" that includes a *Jesus Film* video and an invitation to a new believers class referred to as "Class 100". (This is a repeating six-week class designed to enfold and educate the new believer on the basics of Christianity such as Prayer, the Bible, Jesus, etc.).

Skeptics and the spiritually curious are also encouraged to visit the "Tell Me More" table. There, seekers are offered a complimentary copy of *More Than a Carpenter* by Josh McDowell. Additional resources such a copies of the *May I Ask You a Question* gospel tract are also available. As a result, SBC is experiencing new convert growth on a weekly basis and an increased attendance in the class for new believers by simply being obedient to the Great Commission via a culturally acceptable evangelistic vehicle.

Matthew Parties

Xenos Christian Fellowship began in 1970 as a student newspaper—The Fish, printed in a boarding house by some Ohio State University students. Founded by Dennis McCallum and Gary DeLashmutt: both were

---

[159] This has now been further simplified by having them visit the information booth.

new converts who liked Jesus and Christianity but were very turned off by the bureaucracy of the "organized religion" they found in the churches they visited. Since it was during the "anti-establishment" phase of the early seventies they decided to start a Bible study that would help other students discover Jesus Christ as the key to meeting humanities problems. The ministry continued to multiply and in 1982, they became the Xenos Christian Fellowship and incorporated as a non-denominational evangelical church.

Appropriately, Xenos (Greek for sojourner) was chosen to remind them that they are sojourners in a foreign land. This church quite possibly may be the first to have specifically geared its outreach methodologies with the postmodern culture in mind. The vast majority of the church's outreach is conducted through their small group (home fellowships, cell groups) ministries. Specifically, they (small groups) regularly (once a month) and strategically have parties in which they invite non-believers to participate. They like to refer to this as "warm evangelism". The goal is to simply befriend the lost community and introduce them to others in the small group.

Another method used by the groups is what they call "Conversation Cuisine". Non-believers are invited to a theme dinner (e.g. Luau) and to participate in a structured conversation on a culturally relevant event (e.g. cloning). Formal invitations are sent out with the stipulation that all opinions are invited and welcome as long as they are not presented in an "obnoxious" way.

It should be pointed out that Xenos views their cell groups as essential for being able to provide a community for reaching the postmodern with the Gospel. In fact, they model themselves from the house church concept in Acts and they take it very seriously. So seriously, that all small group leaders are required to graduate from their "Wednesday Night Seminary." Basically, Xenos offers a low-level seminary every Wednesday and graduation is a prerequisite for small group leaders who essentially are "lay pastors". The classes are divided into five categories. "Christian Principles" is a one-year class that primarily focuses on systematic theology. "Servanthood" is for 20 weeks and is geared towards practical ministry experience. "Leadership" is the next step and goes for 10 weeks. Step four is ten Bible classes on topics like Hermeneutics, Homiletics, Apologetics, etc. Finally, there are a series of required seminars on community development, missions, etc. Graduates then are eligible for becoming pastors, teachers, and small group leaders. While visiting there I was surprised and encouraged at the demographic make-up of the Wednesday Night training. Most were in their mid 20s and if you didn't know otherwise you'd think that you were on the campus of the community college.

Xenos is a very cerebral church but as the leaders will tell you, the church is driven through building community via the house churches. "Postmodern people, it is agreed, are group-oriented"[160] and Xenos has been able to capitalize on this dynamic. Although Xenos doesn't consider itself to be a "meta-church", they are a large church that has been strategically broken down into small groups for the purpose of building effective, transparent, and personal communities that intentionally enfold the postmodernist.

---

[160] Veith, *Postmodern Times*, p. 227.

Chapter 13

Utilizing The Personal Testimony

One of the more effective methodologies for sharing the gospel with a postmodernist is the personal testimony. Just like the blind man of John 9, no one can really dispute the fact that we were once spiritually blind, but now we see. It also serves to fight fire with fire because it allows the believer to express what works for them personally. Interestingly, the blind man of John 9 refused to enter into a theological debate with the Pharisees. Rather, he spoke directly from his own experience and was able to say with confidence that "One thing I do know. I was blind but now I see!" (Jn. 9:25).

Although it is very helpful, it is not always necessary that one must first establish the trustworthiness, reliability, and authority of Scripture prior to presenting the Good News.[161] Please understand that I believe in the inerrancy, inspiration, and authority of Scripture as God's revelation and that it is sharper than a two edged sword (Heb. 4:12). I am pro-Bible. Rather, I am simply suggesting that the evangelistic process for

---

[161] This approach is similar to the "One-Step" methodology that is utilized in Apologetics. For an example see Gary Habermas's use of the Resurrection in *Five Views on Apologetics*.

communicating the gospel to a postmodernist does not always necessitate that we must *first* convince them of Scripture's credibility. In fact, it may not begin until post-conversion.

Postmodernism means that more attention will have to be given to the concept of pre-evangelism.

> Christian evangelism must not assume that unbelievers come to the table with any understanding of the nature of God, Christ, sin, eternity, or their own souls. In our attempt to rationally and lovingly persuade people to embrace Jesus Christ as the only way of spiritual liberation, we must be sure to accurately explain and illustrate our own terms. In other words, a great deal of pre-evangelism is usually needed at the level of the nature of truth and its implications on life, since postmodernist thought is so confused on these matters.[162]

Being able to articulate the conversion experience and spiritual journey is possibly the most effective vehicle for postmodern evangelism. This can be accomplished in a very simplistic three-step process that teaches the participant to articulate what their spiritual life was like before Christ; their conversion experience; and finally, what their life has been like since. This sequence provides an easy to remember outline that is personal and graspable.

Most Generation X-ers enjoy hearing personal stories. This is especially the case if it is authentic and transparent.

> To present a picture of Christ that busters can relate to, we need to rely on the power of story. Busters have never read the Bible, and unlike boomers, they don't care what *Time* magazine or other experts have to say. But they will listen to your story, especially if it honestly describes the difficult as well as the

---

[162] Douglas Groothuis, *Truth Decay*, p. 274.

good aspects of following Christ. They will listen to the story of someone who hasn't necessarily been successful, but has been faithful. Storytelling is the most effective way to reach this generation, because busters will not argue with a person's story. *In fact, it may be their only absolute*: (italics mine) Everyone's story is worth listening to and hearing from. Here's what needs to be communicated: 'God's story intersected with my story; now I can share it with you so that you can consider making it a part of your story'.[163]

A concise and well thought-out description of a believer's spiritual journey can have a powerful impact upon the postmodernist.[164] For one, they tend to appreciate authenticity and secondly they still place value in what works. Therefore, its imperative that the believer's character be Christ-like in order for the next component to be applicable.

---

[163] Dieter Zander, , "The Gospel for Generation X" in *Growing Your Church through Evangelism and Outreach*, p. 56. "Buster" is synonymous with Generation X.

[164] "It is (my) conclusion that story telling discussions provide an easy and effective way for Christians to engage their non-Christian friends with the claims of Christ and the gospel." *Training Christians to Reach Secular People Through the Use of Biblical Stories* (D. Min. diss., by David James O'Leary, Covenant Theological Seminary, 1995).

Chapter 14

Building Relationships

The proposition that Christians need to intentionally develop friendships with unbelievers sounds cliché, canned, and obvious. Nevertheless, overuse does not negate its impact and effectiveness.[165] This was the primary thesis behind Rebecca Manley Pippert's popular book that was released in 1979 entitled *Out of the Saltshaker & Into the World* in which she emphasized the concept of friendship evangelism for reaching the un-churched with the gospel. Mark Mittelberg says, "As I've had the privilege of teaching and doing evangelism all over the world, I've observed a consistent human dynamic in every culture I've been to: *Friends listen to friends.* People are growing increasingly suspicious of strangers, sales pitches, and institutional authorities."[166] The postmodern doesn't even want relatives and friends knocking on their door on a Saturday morning unannounced, much less a couple of proselytizers.

---

[165] George Hunter attributes "relational evangelism" as one of the key components for the success of Patrick's mission. He was trusted because he was seen as one of them and as one who sincerely cared about their welfare and thus he earned the right to be heard. See *The Celtic Way of Evangelism* (Nashville: Abingdom Press, 2000).

[166] Mittelberg, *Building A Contagious Church*, p. 70.

The Barna Report presented statistics demonstrating that more than three times as many people came to faith through the personal witness of a friend than through hearing the gospel preached in a church. The ratio went up to almost ten times as many reached by friends as by evangelistic events or crusades alone.[167] "Postmodern evangelism also can be summarized in one word: relationships. According to the Billy Graham Evangelistic Association, 80% of adults coming to faith in Jesus Christ do so as a result of the influence of a friend."[168] (Large-scale evangelism will continue to have its place, but the fundamental and biblical place to begin is on the personal level. Furthermore, the majority of nonbelievers who visit large-scale evangelistic events attend because a Christian friend had extended the invitation).

Dieter Zander, says:

> Busters process truth better relationally than propositionally. Evangelism at New Song happened through bicycle trips, hikes, and mountain climbs. To reach busters means someone needs to spend time with them, someone who feels comfortable sharing why he or she became a Christian, someone willing to expose the work of life in his or her life. This approach is labor intensive, so its more important than ever for pastors to empower people on the front lines. It is the church members who will help their friends cross that line of commitment to Christ.[169]

---

[167] George Barna, *The Barna Report*, vol 1, no. 1, 1996.

[168] Leonard Sweet, *SoulTsunami*, (Grand Rapids: Zondervan, 1999), p. 196.

[169] Marshall Shelley, *Growing Your Church Through Evangelism and Outreach*, "The Gospel for Generation X" by Dieter Zander, p. 56. Prior to serving at WCC, Zander planted New Song Church in San Dimas, California which was specifically designed to minister to Generation X. Some practical ideas on friendship evangelism can be found in *The Joy of Hospitality: Fun Ideas for Evangelistic Entertaining* by Vonette Bright, *Parties with Purpose: Laying the Groundwork Discipleship and Evangelism* by Marlene LeFever, and in "Maximizing Outreach Around the Interpersonal Style" (chapter 13) of *Building a Contagious Church* by Mark Mittelberg.

One of the easiest ways to accomplish this is to simply start inviting non-believers to attend events and activities that you are already participating in. Include a non-believer in your foursome, join a tennis league for the express purpose of meeting and befriending pagans, invite an unchurched couple to join you for dinner, to your Sunday school class Christmas party, etc., etc. The possibility that they will begin to notice something different about you and your Christian friends is towering. Pray for them and don't be surprised if *they* are the ones that begin to seek you out for spiritual conversations and questions.

> "The most effective means of getting people to experience what a church has to offer is having someone they know who belongs to the church simply invite them to try it-this is indisputably the most effective means of increasing church rolls."
> —George Barna,
> *Marketing the Church*

Chapter 15

Getting Global, Getting Local

Many of the themes that we now struggle against in the United States were the same issues that missionaries of the past dealt with when they went to evangelize foreign countries and cultures. Postmodernism has allowed "world religions" to find a home in North America. Although there has always been a general plurality of religious beliefs, a closer interaction between people of different faiths is much more common today than ever before in the United States. Robert Nash, Jr., Assistant Professor of Religion at Shorter College in Rome, Georgia says, "(Today) people treat religions like winter coats they can put on or take off depending on the changes in the weather. They dabble for awhile in a Baptist or Methodist church, check out Presbyterianism or Catholicism, and experiment with Eastern forms of meditation. In the process, Christianity is quickly being marginalized as merely one among a number of religious perspectives."[170]

---

[170] Robert Nash Jr., *An 8-Track Church in a CD World* (Macon GA: Smyth & Helwys, 1997), p.7. Richard Cimino has authored a book entitled *Shopping for Faith* (San Francisco: Jossey Bass, 1998) in which he demonstrates how United States citizens have become so accustomed to the consumer driven culture that they now shop for

The abundance of religion in a multicultural environment has made non-Western beliefs more readily accessible. "In a tolerant age, one is free to create a faith of one's own...Spirituality becomes more of a consumer item than a matter of facts."[171]

Additionally, immigration has brought otherwise non-Western beliefs into our community.[172] Therefore, in order to truly adopt a missional ethos, the local church needs to understand the beliefs of the culture it seeks to evangelize. Because of plurality this means that we need to at least have a general understanding of some of the more popular beliefs such as Buddhism and Eastern thought. Lesslie Newbigin remarks, "It has become commonplace to say that we live in a pluralistic society-not merely a society which is in fact plural in the variety of cultures, religions and lifestyles which it embraces, but pluralist in the sense that this plurality is celebrated as things to be approved and cherished."[173]

The authors of *Complete Idiot's Guide to World Religions* reflect the postmodern sentiment when they say, "If there was ever a time in human history when a nonjudgmental, curious, and open-minded approach to the religions of other people was an advantage, this is that time."[174] Religious diversity has indeed become a reality of our culture, and being able to

---

religions in the same way they look for any other product. Of particular interest is the fact that they tend to shop more for what's convenient without necessarily adopting all of the religion's dogmas and they prefer the spiritual experience over the religious ideologies.

[171] Douglas Groothuis, *Truth Decay* (Downers Grove, IL: InterVarsity Press, 2000), p. 28.

[172] According to the *1999 World Almanac*, in the U.S. there are nearly as many Hindu practitioners as there are Orthodox Jews, more Buddhists than Seventh Day Adventists, and more Muslims than Episcopalians.

[173] Lesslie Newbigin, *The Gospel in a Pluralistic World* (Grand Rapids: Eerdmans, 1989), p. 1.

[174] *The Complete Idiot's Guide to World Religions*, editors Brandon Toropov and Father Luke Buckles (New York: Alpha Books, 1997), p. 3.

build bridges to those who profess allegiance to other faiths is essential, because the more we know about the beliefs of other faiths, the more respect we will gain from our hearers, and we will have less fear when interacting with them.

Paul Griffiths and Delmas Lewis said, "It is both logically and practically possible for us, as Christians, to respect and revere worthy representatives of other traditions while still believing-on rational grounds-that some aspects of their worldview are simply mistaken."[175] Paul illustrated this skill well in his discourse on Mars Hill that is recorded in Acts 17 in which he was able to use his knowledge of their poets, philosophers, and religion to build common ground as a platform for presenting the Gospel.[176]

In spite of their espousal for plurality it appears that religion to the postmodernist is more of a hobby rather than a serious way of life. As Os Guiness said, "Religion is no longer transcendent, but a recreational pursuit for the connoisseurs of spirituality."[177] Nevertheless, being able to demonstrate a basic understanding in other beliefs shows that we are not myopic or tunnel-visioned and thus adds some credibility to our spiritual journey. Personally, it has been my experience that most postmodernists rarely actually practice any religious belief and even an elementary understanding of other faiths is sufficient to engage intelligently in a spiritual conversation regarding other religious beliefs.

---

[175] Paul Griffiths & Delmas Lewis, "On Grading Religions, Seeking Truth, and Being Nice to People: A Reply to Professor Hick", *Religious Studies* 19 (1983): 78.

[176] In (Acts 17:23) Paul utilizes the statue "To An Unknown God" to initiate a spiritual discourse. Regarding (Acts 17:28), "There are two quotations here: (1) 'In him we live and move and have our being,' from the Cretan poet Epimenides (c. 600 BC) in his *Cretica*, and (2) 'We are his offspring,' from the Cilician poet Aratus (c. 315-240) in his *Hymn to Zeus*." *NIV Study Bible* (Grand Rapids: Zondervan, 1995), p. 1683. Paul quotes Greek poets elsewhere as well (see 1 Cor 15:33 and Titus 1:12.

[177] Os Guiness, *The American Hour* (New York: Free Press, 1992), p. 129.

Act Locally

This is also a good time for us to start thinking about ministry that is outside of our constituency. A pastor friend of mine in the San Francisco area was asked by a rather hostile resident within the vicinity of the church as to what deemed his church to be eligible for non-profit status. That is, the neighbor wanted to know: "What is your church doing for the community that doesn't belong to your church? Or do you only minister to your own constituents?" This is an area of opportunity for the North American church at large to focus a little more time and energy towards. For one, it is biblical. The ministry of Jesus Christ obviously exhibited a holistic approach towards ministry. It also earns us the right to be heard within our community and it removes many of the stereotypical assumptions that postmoderns have regarding Christianity.

If your church is already actively involved with a holistic ministry that is focused on the homeless, incarcerated, less fortunate, etc. encourage your volunteers and make these ministries more visible. If you presently do not have such a ministry consider partnering with a non-profit ministry that will enable your members to experience and participate in holistic ministry.

WWW.

Is your church on the web? Do you have your own website? It is imperative that you have both in order to do ministry to a postmodern culture. If you want to be able to speak postmodernese and communicate to your culture you need to be able to so via cyberspace. The possibilities are absolutely endless. Here is a vehicle that the church can use to communicate the transforming power of Jesus Christ to the entire world. Many postmoderns will evaluate your church based upon the quality of your website. IF you don't have one, you're not even in the game. Likewise, you should have your own personal web page (you can get these for free from sites like yahoo.com and geocities.com) and include a link to your church's home page. Include the gospel in postmodernese on both.

If you don't know how to do the above, learn. Sign up for a class. The investment is well worth it and as necessary as learning Spanish if you were going to minister in Latin America. Find a volunteer at your church to get your website online. Millions of people are already surfing the web and soon the number will go into the billions. Will you be there to communicate the gospel and spiritual truths to them via their preferred language? If you and your church want to reach postmoderns you absolutely must get online.

Conclusion

Christianity is alive and well in the minds and hearts of countless believers. And, according to author Paul Johnson, "all the evidence suggests that Christianity will still be flourishing another thousand years from now, for it continues to strike new roots and regain lost territories."[178] The largest evangelical church in the world is in South Korea. (In 1900 there were virtually no evangelical churches there). In West Africa, Christians whose ancestors were pagans two centuries ago, have built one of the largest churches in the world, roughly the size of St. Peter's in Rome. In Russia, the building that once housed the Museum of Religion and Atheism is now a church of the Orthodox Christian faith. Evangelical Catholicism is spreading in South Africa and Protestant evangelicalism is spreading in Latin America. Some people are speculating that Guatemala may become the first Latin Christian nation with a Christian population of 51%.

In some ways we can see the glass as being half full in regards to postmodernism. In many ways postmodern Christians are not far from the first century Christians, and we could view America as a pre-Christian culture. The most recent statistics from the polls of George Gallup Jr. (and George Barna) indicate that the vast majority of Americans (96%) believe in God and most (89%) believe that there is a God watching over us who answers prayer?[179] Eighty-four percent believe that Jesus Christ is God.[180]

---

[178] *Reader's Digest,* "Whose Millennium?" December, 1999, p. 64.

[179] George Gallup Jr., *The New American Spirituality* (Colorado Springs: Victor Books, 2000), p. 177.

[180] *Ibid*, p. 177.

Americans are seeking ways to reestablish a connection to vital faith and unlike any situation before in the course of human history, we have literally set a trap due to the incredible amount of resources available to the follower of Jesus Christ in the United States. Leonard Sweet refers to this spiritual hunger within postmodern culture as a "spiritual tsunami." This wave, he says, "will build without breaking for decades to come."[181]

"Evangelism then must be based on the longing to share the good news of God with a world that sorely needs hope and forgiveness, and on a fundamental conviction of the truth of the gospel. It springs from a deep feeling of love and a heartfelt desire to share something wonderful and trustworthy, something that would be selfish and irresponsible to keep to oneself."[182] We must proclaim the profound attractiveness of faith to the world, in the full and confident expectation that the gospel is inherently applicable, relevant, and life changing.

Evangelism makes little sense unless there is a real and passionate conviction concerning the uniqueness of Christ, his atoning work on the cross and the need for a personal response of faith from those who hear the gospel message. "Classical Christianity was shaped in a pagan and relativistic society much like our own. (It) was not an accommodation to paganism but an alternative practice to life. Christians in a postmodern world will succeed not by watering down the faith, but by being a countercultural community that invites people to be shaped by the story of Jesus."[183] Outreach methodologies for the local church must begin to be implemented with the postmodernist in mind while remaining doctrinally, biblically, and theologically sound. It is no exaggeration to suggest that the future of Christianity's growth in the suburbs of the local church will depend on this continuing motivation.

---

[181] Leonard Sweet, *SoulTsunami* (Grand Rapids: Zondervan, 1999), p. 420.
[182] Alister McGrath, *Evangelicalism & the Future of Christianity*, p. 163.
[183] Robert Webber, *Ancient-Future Faith*, p. 7.

Bibliography

Appignanesi, Richard. *Introducing Postmodernism.* New York: Totem Books, 1995.

Barna, George. *Marketing the Church.* Colorado Springs, Navpress, 1988.

Bork, Robert. *Slouching Towards Gomorrah.* Grand Rapids: Eerdmans, 1991.

Bosch, David. *Believing in the Future.* Harrisburg, PA: Trinity Press, 1995.

_____. *Transforming Mission: Paradigm Shifts in Theology of Mission.* New York: Orbis Books, 1991.

Boyack, Kenneth. *Catholic Evangelization Today: A New Pentecost for the United States.* New York: Paulist Publishers, 1987.

Brierley, Peter. *Future Church.* London: Monarch Books, 1998.

Brown, Dee. *Bury My Heart at Wounded Knee: An Indian History of the American West.* New York: Bantam Books, 1971.

Callahan, Kenneth. *Effective Church Leadership.* San Francisco: Jossey-Bass Publishers, 1990).

Christianity Today, "Downtown Evangelism Makes A Comeback", January, 2001.

Choosing the Right College. Grand Rapids: Eerdmans, 1998.

Cimino, Richard. *Shopping for Faith.* San Francisco: Jossey-Bass Publishers, 1998.

Colson, Charles. *How Now Shall We Live?* Wheaton: Tyndale House Publishers, 1999.

Complete Idiot's Guide to World Religions. New York: Alpha Books, 1997.

Constanzo, William. *Reading the Movies.* Urbana, IL.: National Council of Teachers, 1992.

Coplestone, F.C. *A History of Philosophy.* New York: Avon Books, 1985.

Cruickshank, John. *Albert Camus and the Literature of Revolt.* New York: Oxford Univ. Press, 1960.

Deleuze, Gilles. *The Clamor of Being.* Minneapolis: Univ. of Minn. Press, 1999.

_____, and Guattari, Felix. *A Thousand Plateaus.* Minneapolis: Univ. of Minn. Press, 1998.

Denzin, Norman. *Images of Postmodern Society.* Newberry Park, CA.: Sage Publications, 1991.

Derrida, Jacques. *Of Grammatology.* Baltimore: Johns Hopkins Univ. Press, 1976.

Eble, Kenneth. *The Craft of Teaching.* San Francisco: Jossey-Bass, 1994.

Engel, James. *Changing the Mind of Missions.* Downer's Grove, IL.: InterVarsity Press, 2000.

Erickson, Millard. *Christian Theology, 2nd Edition.* Grand Rapids: Baker Books, 1998.

Evangelical Dictionary of Biblical Theology, editor Walter Elwell. Grand Rapids: Baker 1996.

Faye, Bill. *Share Jesus Without Fear.* Nashville: LifeWay Press, 1997.

Feyerband, Paul. *Farewell to Reason.* New York: Verso, 1987.

Foucalt, Michel. *Power/Knowledge.* New York: Pantheon Books, 1972.

_____, "Strategies of Power" in *The Truth About Truth:De-confusing and Reconstructing the Postmodern World,* ed. Walter Truett Anderson. New York G.P. Putnam's Sons, 1995, p. 45.

Friedrich, Gerhard. *Theological Dictionary of the New Testament, vol. 2.* Grand Rapids: Eerdmans, 1976.

Gallup, Jr., George. *American Spirituality.* Colorado Springs: Cook Publications, 2000.

Geisler, Norman. *Baker Encyclopedia of Apologetics.* Grand Rapids: Baker Books, 1999.

Grenz, Stanley. *A Primer on Postmodernism.* Grand Rapids, Eerdmans, 1996.

Groothuis, Douglas. *Truth Decay.* Downers Grove, IL: InterVarsity Press, 2000.

Grudem, Wayne. Editor, *Are Miraculous Gifts for Today.* Grand Rapids: Zondervan, 1996.

Guder, Darrell. *The Continuing Conversion of the Church.* Grand Rapids: Eerdmans, 2000.

Guiness, Os. *The American Hour.* New York: Free Press, 1992.

Hanegraaff, Hank. *The Face that Demonstrates the Farce of Evolution.* Nashville: Word Publishing, 1998.

Harvey, David. *The Condition of Postmodernity.* Oxford: Blackwell Publishing, 1989.

Henderson, David. *Culture Shift.* Grand Rapids: Baker Books, 1998.

Hengel, Martin. *Between Jesus and Paul: Studies in the Earliest History of Christianity*, trans. John Bowden. Philadelphia: Fortress, 1983.

Henry, Matthew. *Matthew Henry's Commentary in One Volume.* Grand Rapids: Zondervan, 1960.

Hertig, Paul. The Galilee Theme in Matthew: "Transforming Mission through Marginality" in *Missiology*, vol. 25, 1997.

Hybels, Bill. *Becoming A Contagious Christian.* Grand Rapids: Zondervan, 1995.

Indian Missiological Review (February, 1986).

Hodges, Zane. *The Gospel Under Siege*. Dallas: Redencion Viva, 1981.

_____. *Absolutely Free*. Dallas: Redencion Viva, 1989.

Hull, Bill. *Can We Save the Evangelical Church?* Grand Rapids: Revell, 1993.

Hunter, George. *Church for the Unchurched*. Nashville: Abingdon, 1996.

Hunter, James Davison. *Evangelicalism: The Coming Generation*. Chicago: Univ. of Chicago Press, 1987.

Hybels, Bill. *Becoming A Contagious Christian*. Grand Rapids: Zondervan, 1994.

Kennedy, D. James. *Evangelism Explosion*, 4th ed. Wheaton: Tyndale, 1983.

Knoke, William. *Bold New World*. New York: Kondansha, 1996.

Laurie, Greg. *How to Share Your Faith*. Wheaton: Tyndale House, 1999.

Long, Jimmy. *Generating Hope: A Strategy for Reaching the Postmodern Generation*. Downers Grove: InterVarsity Press, 1997.

Lowman, Joseph. *Mastering the Techniques of Teaching*. San Francisco: Jossey-Bass, 1994.

Lyotard, Jean-Francois. *The Postmodern Condition: A Report on Knowledge*. Minneapolis: Univ. of Minnesota Press, reprint, 1975.

_____. *The Postmodern Explained.* Minneapolis: Univ. of Minnesota Press, 1978.

MacArthur, Jr., John. *The Gospel According to Jesus.* Grand Rapids: Zondervan, 1988.

MacIntyre, After Virtue: *A Study in Moral Theory*, 2nd ed. Notre Dame, IN: Univ. of Notre Dame Press, 1984.

McCallum, Dennis. *The Death of Truth.* Minneapolis: Bethany House Publishers, 1996.

McGrath, Alister. *Evangelicalism & the Future of Christianity.* Chicago: InterVarsity Press, 1995.

_____. *A Passion for Truth.* Downers Grove, IL, 1996.

McKeachie, Wilbert. *Teaching Tips: Strategies, Research, and Theory for College and University Teachers.* Boston: Houghton-Mifflin Co., 1984.

Mitchell, Susan. *American Generations.* Ithaca, NY.: New Strategist Publications, 1998.

Mittelberg, Mark. *Building A Contagious Church.* Grand Rapids: Zondervan, 2000.

Miller, Perry. *Errand to the Wilderness.* Cambridge, MA.: Harvard Univ. Press, 1956.

Moyer, Larry. *Free and Clear.* Grand Rapids: Kregel Publications, 1997.

Naisbitt, John. *Megatrends 2000.* New York: Avon Books, 1990.

Nash Jr., Robert. *An 8-Track Church in a CD World.* Macon GA.: Smyth & Helwys, 1997.

Neill, Stephen. *The Church and the Christian Union.* London: Oxford Univ. Press, 1968.

Newbigin, Lesslie. *Foolishness to the Greeks.* Grand Rapids: Eerdmans, 1986.

_____, *The Gospel in a Pluralistic Society.* Grand Rapids: Eerdmans, 1989.

Newsweek, "Searching for the Holy Spirit" (May 8, 2000).

Nietzsche, Friederick, "Truth and the Extra-Moral Sense," in *The Portable Nietzsche*, Walter Kauffman, ed. New York: Viking, 1968.

Okholm, Dennis & Phillips, Timothy. Editors. *Four Views on Salvation in a Pluralistic World.* Grand Rapids: Zondervan, 1997.

O' Leary, David James. "Training Christians to Reach Secular People Through Biblical Studies" (D. Min. diss., Covenant Theological Seminary, 1995).

Osborne, Richard. *Philosophy for Beginners.* New York: Writers & Readers, 1995.

Pfeiffer, Charles; Rea, John; and Vos, Howard, Editors, *Wycliffe Bible Dictionary.* Chicago: Moody Press, 1999.

Posehn, Keith. "Getting Baby Busters to Church: Attracting and Integrating Baby Busters into the Life and Worship of the Local

Church." (D. Min. diss., Austin Presbyterian Theological Seminary, 1997).

Powell, Jim. *Postmodernism for Beginners*. New York: Writers & Readers Inc., 1998.

Romanowski, William. *Pop Culture Wars: Religion & the Role of Entertainment in American Life*. Downer's Grove, IL.: InterVarsity Press, 1966.

Sartre, Jean-Paul. *Nausea*. New York: W.W. Norton & Co., 1975.

_____, *Words*. New York: Vintage, 1981.

Schaeffer, Francis. *The God Who is There*. Downer's Grove: InterVarsity Press, 1969.

Schultz, Thom & Joani. *Why Nobody Learns Anything at Church*. Loveland, CO: Group Publishing, 1993.

Shaw, R. Daniel. "In Search of Postmodern Salvation" in *Evangelical Review of Theology*, (vol. 22, 1998).

Shelley, Marshall. *Growing Your Church Through Evangelism and Outreach*. Nashville: Moorings, 1996.

Sire, James. *The Universe Next Door*. Downers Grove: InterVarsity Press, 1976.

Smith, Chuck, Jr. *The End of the World As We Know It*. Colorado Springs: WaterBook Press. 2001.

Sproul, R.C. *Faith Alone.* Grand Rapids: Baker Books, 1995.

Story, Dan. *Engaging the Closed Mind.* Grand Rapids: Kregel Publications, 1999.

Strobel, Lee. *The Case for Faith.* Grand Rapids: Zondervan, 2000.

Stumpf, Samuel. *Socrates to Sartre vol. 4.* New York: McGraw-Hill, 1988.

Sweet, Leonard. *Aqua Church.* Loveland, CO: Group Publishing, 1999.

_____. *Carpe Manana.* Grand Rapids, MI: Zondervan, 2001.

_____. *Postmodern Pilgrims.* Nashville: Broadman & Holman, 2000.

Van Engen, Charles. "Mission Theology in the Light of Postmodern Critique," *International Review of Mission*, vol. LXXXVI, No. 343, October, 1997.

Van Gelder, Craig. *The Church Between Gospel and Culture.* Grand Rapids: Eerdmans, 1996.

Veith Jr., Robert. *Postmodern Times.* Wheaton: Crossway Books, 1994.

Warren, Rick. *The Purpose Driven Church.* Grand Rapids: Zondervan, 1995.

Webber, Robert. *Ancient-Future Faith.* Grand Rapids: Baker Books, 1999.

Wegner, Paul D. *The Journey from Texts to Translations: The Origin and Development of the Bible.* Grand Rapids: Baker Books, 1999.

Wells, David. *No Place for Truth*. Grand Rapids: Eerdmans, 1993.

Websters New World Dictionary. Nashville: Nelson Publishers, 1989.

Appendix: What is the Gospel?

Because we have made some poor choices and mistakes (what the Bible calls sin) in life we have missed the standard that God has set for us. As a result of sin we are separated from God. There is no way that we can earn or merit everlasting life, but the Good News is that God has initiated peace with us. This is why (in the Christmas Story) an Angel of the Lord told the shepherds "I bring you good news of great joy which shall be for all people. Today…a Savior has been born to you; He is Christ the Lord" (Luke 2: 10–11). This Savior (Rescuer) was Jesus. Since He is God, He alone has the credentials to offer forgiveness and everlasting life.

Imagine you had cancer cells in your body that were slowly but surely killing you, yet there was a medical way in which we could extract all of your cancer cells and place them into my body. What would happen to you? You would live. But, what would happen to me? I would then die. The truth of the matter is that all of humanity has a sin virus, but unlike cancer it has eternal repercussions. The Good News is that Jesus has offered to remove these "sin cells" in order that you can have everlasting life. This is what Christians call "born again." The Bible says that Jesus took the penalty for our sins and placed it upon Himself when He was crucified on the Cross. "God demonstrates His own love toward us, in that while we were yet sinners, Christ died for us" (Rom. 5:8).

The Good News is that because Jesus is God He rose again three days later after being crucified demonstrating His victory over sin and death. That is why to this day Christians celebrate Easter. Therefore, if you are willing to ask Jesus to forgive you for your sins and to place your faith in Him alone for your salvation, rather than in works, you too can be born again. The Bible says, "For by grace you have been saved through faith, and not of yourselves; it is the gift of God, not of works, that no one should boast" (Ephesians 2:8, 9).

Would you like to tell God that you are sorry for your sins and turn your life over to Him? If yes, in your own words pray the following:

"Dear God, I know that I am a sinner. I am so sorry for my sins and know that I deserve death. I believe that Jesus died for my sins and rose from the grave. I trust you now for my salvation. Thank you for forgiveness and everlasting life. In Jesus name, amen."

Remember that its not the prayer that saves you, but trusting in Jesus for your forgiveness and salvation that saves you.

Now what? Tell another Christian that you are born again. Begin to read the Bible (start with the book of John in the New Testament). Begin to spend time in prayer and find other believers to fellowship and worship with. Drop me an email and I'd be glad to answer your questions on getting started (bbrewer@sbcaz.org).

About the Author

Dr. Robert "Bobby" Brewer is Pastor of Community Outreach and Church Growth at Scottsdale Bible Church, Scottsdale, Arizona.

D. Min., Phoenix Seminary; M.Div., Liberty Baptist Theological Seminary; B.S., Religion, Liberty University (Lynchburg, Virginia).

For more info visit www.postmodernoutreach.net and www.scottsdalebible.com

Other books by the Author
Co-Author, *Ask Pastor Darryl: Answers to 121 Frequently Asked Bible Questions*. Contact Scottsdale Bible Church for a copy or email bbrewer@sbcaz.org.

0-595-25372-5